Disney's

ART OF ANIMATION

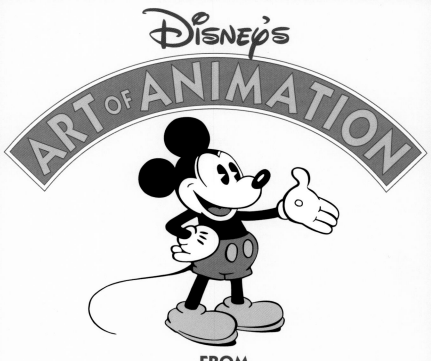

FROM
MICKEY MOUSE
TO
HERCULES

By Bob Thomas

A WELCOME BOOK

HYPERION

NEW YORK

For information address
HYPERION
114 Fifth Avenue, New York, New York 10011.

Produced by
WELCOME ENTERPRISES, INC.
575 Broadway, New York, New York 10012

SECOND EDITION
Project Directors: Ellen Mendlow, Jonathan Glick
Project Manager: Jacqueline Véissid
Designer: Tim Shaner
Hyperion Editor: Wendy Lefkon
Editorial Assistant: Monique Peterson

Library of Congress Cataloging-in-Publication Data
Thomas, Bob, 1992-
Disney's Art of animation : from Mickey Mouse to Hercules / by Bob Thomas. — 1st ed.
p.   cm.
"A Welcome book."
Includes index.
ISBN 0-7868-6241-6
1. Walt Disney Productions.   2. Animated films—Technique. I. Title.
II. Title: Art of animation
NC1766.U52D568 1997
741.5'8' 0979493—dc20   96-9204
                                                             CIP

SECOND EDITION
2 4 6 8 10 9 7 5 3 1

Printed and bound in Singapore by Toppan Printing Co., Inc.

HISTORY OF A NEW ART

THE MAKING OF HERCULES

To My Grandsons
Matthew Clayton Goff
Ryan Thomas McGowan

ACKNOWLEDGMENTS

Walt Disney said to me in 1957: "All these years I've been taking the bows for the cartoons and the animated features. I did that for a purpose: to establish the Disney name as a guarantee to the public of good family entertainment. Now I want to give credit to the guys who made all those pictures."

The result was *The Art of Animation*, a history of animation at the Disney Studio, together with an account of the making of *Sleeping Beauty*. Little had been written about animation at that time, and apparently the book helped a young generation to seek careers in the field.

Now I'm writing about that new generation and the challenge they are making to Disney achievements of the past. Parts of *The Art of Animation* are included in a different form in Chapters 1 through 7. I have also drawn on previously unpublished interviews I did in 1957 with Walt Disney and his artists.

For the second edition—my thanks to Wendy Lefkon of Hyperion for editing and counsel, and the following for interviews, advice, and assistance:

Roger Allers, Lizza Andreas, Rasoul Azadani, Paul and Gaëtan Brizzi, Tom Cardone, Ron Clements, Andreas Deja, Tony DeRosa, Alice Dewey, Roy E. Disney, Ken Duncan, Michael Eisner, Doug Engalla, Brian Ferguson, Tom Finan, Andy Gaskill, Kathleen Gavin, Jon Glick, Dave Goetz, Eric Goldberg, Patrick Golier, Roger Gould, Howard Green, Don Hahn, Jo Haidar, Randy Haycock, Phil Isaacs, Barry Johnson, Nancy Kniep, John Lasseter, Bobby Lee, Tim Lewis, James Lopez, Mauro Maressa, Don McEnery, Irene Mecchi, Alan Menken, Dominique Monfery, Chris Montan, John Musker, Sue Nichols, Monique Peterson, John Pomeroy, Nik Ranieri, Steve Rogers, Gerald Scarfe, Peter Schneider, Russell Schroeder, Thomas Schumacher, Henry Selick, Bob Shaw, Mike Show, Michael Stern, Kevin Susman, Gary Trousdale, Oskar Urretabizkaia, Jacqueline Véissid, Kirk Wise, Ellen Woodbury, and David Zippel.

BOOK ONE
HISTORY OF A NEW ART

CHAPTER ONE
A MOUSE IS BORN

UNIVERSAL
presents
OSWALD
THE
LUCKY RABBIT
IN
"THE OL' SWIMMIN' HOLE"
A Winkler Production
by WALT DISNEY

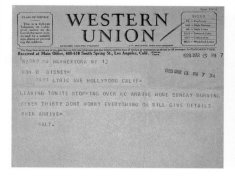

PRECEDING SPREAD: *Mickey Mouse in the 1932* Mickey's Revue *(INSET) and the 1935* The Band Concert *(SPREAD).*

LEFT: *Ub Iwerks during the feverish months of creating Mickey Mouse.*

BELOW: *Story sketches for the 1928 Oswald cartoon* Tall Timber.

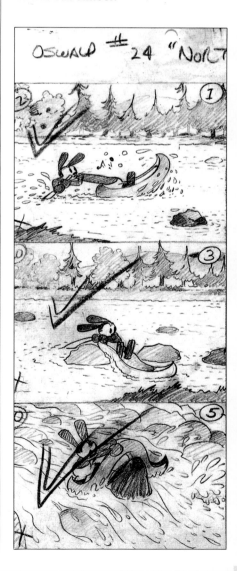

A Star with Two Fathers

Don't worry everything OK
Will give details when arrive
Walt

Walt Disney hid the bitter truth in this telegram to his brother Roy. Everything was not OK. The Disney brothers' enterprise had been shattered by the double-dealing of their New York distributor. Walt had spent February of 1928 in New York trying to renegotiate the contract for his cartoon series Oswald the Lucky Rabbit, hoping to raise the price per cartoon from $2,250 to $2,500. The distributor, Charles Mintz, offered $1,800. "But that's impossible," Walt protested. "We couldn't make a profit."

Then Mintz dropped the bombshell. He declared that he owned all rights to Oswald and warned: "Either you come with me at my price, or I'll take your organization from you. I have your key men signed up."

Walt was desolate. Not only had he lost his star performer, Oswald, he also was being deserted by almost his entire staff, most of whom he had brought to Hollywood from Kansas City. Only his key animator, Ub Iwerks, had remained loyal. Five years before, Disney's Kansas City cartoon studio had gone bankrupt. Now, at 26, he faced the same grim prospect in Hollywood.

How Mickey Mouse was born may never be known. Walt told the story, embellished over the years, that on the train ride back to California he had concocted a new character, based on a friendly mouse who had visited his drawing board back in Kansas City. Ub Iwerks told another version: Walt returned from New

*W*alt told me in 1957: "Mickey had to be simple. We had to push out seven hundred feet of film every two weeks. His head was a circle with an oblong circle for a snout. The ears were also circles so they could be drawn the same, no matter how he turned his head. His body was like a pear, and he had a long tail. His legs were pipestems, and we stuck them in large shoes to give him the look of a kid wearing his father's shoes.

"We didn't want him to have mouse hands, because he was supposed to be more human. So we gave him gloves. [Mickey went gloveless in the first three cartoons.] Five fingers seemed like too much on such a little figure, so we took away one. That was just one less finger to animate.

"To provide a little detail, we gave him the two-button pants. There was no mouse hair, or any other frills that would slow down animation."

ABOVE AND OPPOSITE BOTTOM: Plane Crazy, *the first Mickey Mouse cartoon, was made as a silent, then released in sound after the success of* Steamboat Willie.

TOP: *Model sheets of Mickey* (OPPOSITE) *and Oswald* (RIGHT) *demonstrate the difference in their ear designs.*

York discouraged, and Walt, Roy, and Ub held a meeting to discuss a new character. "How about a cat?" one of them suggested. "No, can't compete with Krazy Kat," another replied. Ub riffled through some magazines, looking for animals. Finally they decided on a mouse. Except for the brick-throwing Ignatz of the Krazy Kat series, mice had been overlooked in cartoons.

Whichever version of Mickey's birth is correct, it is agreed that Walt's wife Lilly did the naming. She rejected the proposal to call the new character Mortimer. "I think he should be called Mickey Mouse," she announced.

The three survivors of the Walt Disney organization had to act fast—and secretly. Walt was obligated to produce three more Oswald cartoons, and the defecting animators would be remaining at the studio for three months. Walt worked up a story line that capitalized on the nation's passion for Charles Lindbergh. Ub began animating *Plane Crazy* in a locked room, surrounded by random sketches. If anyone knocked on the door, he quickly covered up his real work and substituted bogus drawings so the intruder could not see the character that lay aborning on his workbench.

Mickey Mouse was nothing very new; in fact, he bore a strong resemblance to Oswald. Except for the ears. While Oswald's were long and floppy, Mickey's were perfectly round, sitting atop his head.

The simplicity of design was created out of necessity on Ub Iwerks's drawing board. Mickey was essentially a series of circles that permitted Ub to work at superhuman speed. Bill Nolan had held the cartoon industry record for the number of drawings per day: six hundred for Krazy Kat. Ub turned out seven hundred. The entire cartoon consisted of 8,500 drawings.

To maintain the secrecy, Walt set up a little shop in the garage of his house on

MICKEY MOUSE   MODEL Nº1

Lyric Avenue. Lilly, Roy's wife Edna, and Walt's sister-in-law Hazel Sewell inked and painted Ub's drawings onto celluloid.

Plane Crazy previewed well though not sensationally at a Hollywood theater in May 1928, and Walt was encouraged to start another Mickey Mouse cartoon, *Gallopin' Gaucho*. He traveled to New York and engaged a film dealer to sell the new series. But no distributor was interested in cartoons about a mouse, or any other character. Short subjects were a minor part of the movie business, which was now struggling to cope with the talkie revolution.

The Cartoon Finds a Voice

Walt returned to Hollywood without a contract. He called a night meeting at his house with Roy, Ub, and the three remaining loyalists, Les Clark, Wilfred Jackson, and Johnny Cannon.

"Roy, what do you think about trying sound?" Walt began. The entire industry had been thrown into a turmoil the previous October when Warner Bros. introduced sound with Al Jolson in *The Jazz Singer*. Walt continued: "You know they've got the track right on the film now, so you can't get out of sync."

Always the cautious brother, Roy considered the proposal from all aspects. Was sound practical? What would it cost? Was it worth the gamble?

Walt admitted the financial outlook wasn't good. The loss of Oswald had robbed the studio of its income. Walt had mortgaged his home. Many weeks he and Roy didn't get paid, though their employees did.

"I think we ought to do it," Walt decided. "I think sound is here to stay. Think

Studio workers agreed on the symbiotic relationship between Walt and Mickey. First of all, the voice. Out of necessity, Walt uttered Mickey's squeaks in Steamboat Willie. When Mickey began to articulate, Walt auditioned voices. He listened and said impatiently, "No, it's more like this, more like this," and he demonstrated with a Missouri falsetto. Finally his animators said, "Well, Walt, why don't you do it?"

More than the voice, Walt contributed his own adventurousness and sense of wonder to Mickey. In the early years, Walt guided every Mickey Mouse cartoon from beginning to end, and that's when the best of them were made. Animator Frank Thomas observes: "Mickey was Walt, and Walt was Mickey. Mickey reached his height in the days when Walt did the voice in that awful falsetto of his. When he started making feature films, Mickey declined."

ABOVE: *Disney (second from left) and coworkers gag it up to plug the studio's song, "Minnie's Yoo Hoo." Left to right: Johnny Cannon, Walt Disney, Bert Gillett, Ub Iwerks, Wilfred Jackson, and Les Clark; seated, left to right: Carl Stalling, Jack King, and Ben Sharpsteen.*

TOP RIGHT: *Mickey Mouse scripts with Disney's typed continuity and Iwerks's story sketches.*

Scene # 30.

C.U. of Mickey drumming on bucket Old cows head sticking in left side of scene....she is chewing in time to music....she reaches over and licks Mickeys face with her long tongue....then smiles (shows teeth) Mickey sees teeth....opens her mouth wide and hammers on her teeth like playing Xylophone....plays in time to music....runs up and down scale, etc.

Just as he is about to finish two large feet(the Captains) walk into right side of scene and stop....Mickey finishes piece with 'Ta-da-de-da-de-... on cows horns....pulls out her tongue and strums 'Dum - Dum...' on it...and turns around to girl with smile....He sees feet...looks upslowly...when he sees its Captain he acts surprised...

Scene # 2.

Close up of Mickey in cabin of wheel'house, keeping time to last two measures of verse of ' steamboat Bill '. With gesture he starts whistleing the chorus in perfect time to music....his body keeping time with every other beat while his shoulders and foot keep time with each beat. At the end of every two measures he twirls wheel which makes a ratchet sound as it spins. He takes in breath at proper time according to music. When he finishes last measure he reaches up and pulls on whistle cord above his head. (Use FIFE to imitate his whistle)

what we can do with it! Think of how we can use music! Think how much better we can tell stories and put over gags with sound!"

Disney expounded on the values of sound: the gags could be socked across with a well-timed sound effect; the characters would exude more personality if you could hear their voices; the action could be timed to the rhythmic beat of a popular song. Walt put Ub to work on the third Mickey Mouse cartoon, Steamboat Willie, a takeoff on the Buster Keaton comedy Steamboat Bill.

Wilfred Jackson, whose mother had been a piano teacher, devised a way to synchronize music to film by using a metronome. "We know how fast film will run—ninety feet a minute," said Jackson. "All we've got to do is figure how fast the beat of the music is, and we can break it down into frames."

Walt whistled "Steamboat Bill" while Jackson played his harmonica. The metronome ticked out their rhythm. The system worked. But would audiences respond to music and noises emanating from a cartoon? Walt decided to make a test. He invited the workers and their wives to the studio one night. Roy ran the projector outside the window to eliminate sprocket noise. While Steamboat Willie was projected onto a bed sheet, Jackson played his harmonica, Ub and Les Clark beat on boxes and pans, Johnny Cannon made animal sounds, and Walt said a few words of dialogue. The illusion was successful.

Walt next faced the challenge of recording the sound track on the film. He left for New York, stopping in Kansas City to meet Carl Stalling, a theater organist who had helped the Disneys with a much needed $275 loan. Walt persuaded Stalling to compose a score, which was timed to the beat marks Ub had made on the screen.

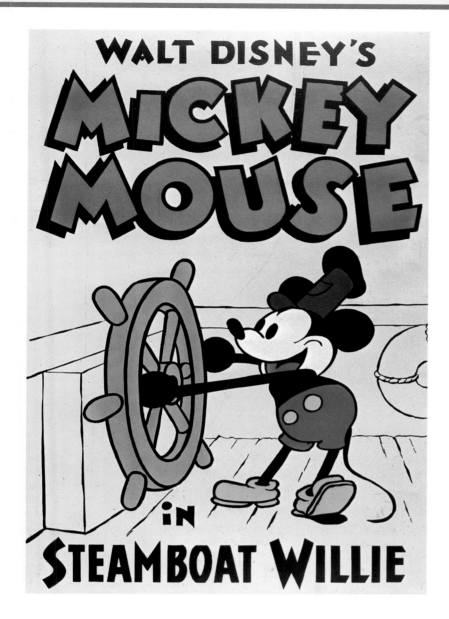

Iwerks's drawings for Steamboat Willie demonstrate the elasticity of *Mickey Mouse.*

Walt continued to New York with the written score and the completed film. The big recording companies were either too busy or too expensive for the young cartoon maker from Hollywood. Walt found a slick operator, Pat Powers, who offered to record *Steamboat Willie* with his own bootlegged equipment.

The first session was a fiasco. The conductor refused to follow the beat marks on the film, and the musicians couldn't keep up with the frantic action on the screen. Walt had already written checks totaling $1,500, which Roy had scrambled to cover. Now Walt decided to sell his Moon roadster to raise more money for a second session. Finally *Steamboat Willie* was recorded, with Walt himself supplying the voices of Minnie and a parrot that shouted, "Man overboard! Man overboard!"

Steamboat Willie had its premiere engagement at the Colony Theater in New York on November 18, 1928. The 7 1/2-minute cartoon drew better reviews than the full-length movies released that week. Critics were delighted with the first sound cartoon. Within weeks, Mickey Mouse was a nationwide sensation. In three years, he would be a national institution.

Story sketches for Orphan's Benefit (1934).
The film was noteworthy for three events:
Dippy Dawg's name was changed to the
permanent and appropriate Goofy; Donald
Duck in his second film made his first featured
appearance, raging as his onstage performance
draws jeers and brickbats; and Clara Cluck
made her Disney debut.
Goofy and Donald went on to vast fame.
Clara's single talent—clucking operatic arias
as a barnyard soprano (voiced by Florence •
Gill)—proved limiting. She appeared in only
seven cartoon shorts, including the 1941 color
remake of Orphan's Benefit.

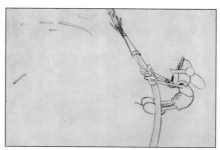

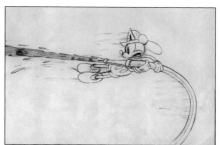

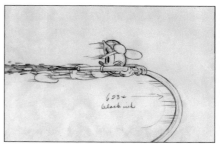

"Remember, He's Just a Mouse"

What was that special alchemy that made audiences around the world respond to Mickey Mouse? Hundreds of theories have been proffered, philosophical and Freudian, profound and crackpot. An intriguing hypothesis is presented by John Hench, who performed several functions in Disney animation beginning in 1939, and remains resident guru of Walt Disney Imagineering, which plans the theme parks.

"I have always been mystified with the power of Mickey Mouse, how he can go everywhere in the world, never to be questioned or suspected of being an American export," says Hench. "It is mostly a matter of déjà vu, apparently, because people seem to recognize something about him."

Hench compares Mickey's appeal to twelve-thousand-year-old fertility symbols that central European tribes carried with them. "They were small stone objects, but they were built on Mickey's formula of hooking together a series of circles—in Mickey's case, spheres—in a dynamic way. He expresses simple ideas: that life is dynamic, that it isn't static. He has this remarkable way of recalling these feelings in people everywhere."

At first, Walt and Ub dreamed up the plots. They sat in the inner office of the tiny studio. Ub drew sketches of the action, and Walt typed the dialogue on the bottom of the sketches, using three fingers on the keyboard. Then he handed them to the animators in the outer office.

Walt soon realized the need to include more minds in the story sessions that were held at night around the dining table in Walt's five-room bungalow. In the center of the table was a film can containing candy.

"How about letting Mickey be a fireman this time?" Walt would propose.

"Good," Ub commented. "Minnie could be caught in a burning building."

TOP LEFT: *The 1941 color remake of* Orphan's Benefit.

ABOVE: *Animation drawings of Mickey in action in* Mickey's Fire Brigade (1935).

As the studio grew, Walt continued seeking ideas from everyone. In 1932 he circulated a two-page synopsis of The Wayward Canary along with this note:

The following story strikes me as having wonderful audience appeal.
This is a wonderful chance for personality stuff with all of the characters.
Special cute action of Mickey and Minnie trying to teach the canary bird to sing.
Pluto trying to sleep with the piano annoying him.
The love making of the two birds.
The villainous looking old cat. (Note this cat is not human—it is carried as a real cat.)
The frantic efforts of Mickey, Minnie and Pluto with the wild canary, all trying to rescue Minnie's bird from the old cat.
Pluto's heroic fight and rescue of the bird.
The happy finish with the entire group bandaged up as they sing and play.
Pluto all bandaged up still trying to sleep—then finally joining in with the tune by howling in goofy manner.
Especially the fight sequence where all four characters are chasing the old cat all over the back yard trying to rescue the little helpless canary.
So let's all hop to it and have some good belly laughs ready by
TUESDAY NIGHT—JUNE 14th

"We could have the ladder slide down the pole and jump on the fire wagon," Jackson suggested. The talk continued far into the night until the script was completed.

More so than any other cartoon character that preceded him, Mickey Mouse remained the same basic, well-defined character in each film. He could adopt a variety of occupations and engage in outrageous adventures, but the steady, well-meaning, straight-shooting Mickey always shone through. Walt saw to that. Story men who engaged in flights of fancy suffered his withering comment: "Mickey wouldn't do that."

Mickey was so much a part of Walt that Walt couldn't articulate what Mickey could and could not do. That was spelled out by a story man in 1939:

Mickey is not a clown; he is neither silly nor dumb. . . . He can be funny in a variety of situations. . . . His first successes were hero roles, such as *Cactus Kid*, *Gorilla Mystery*, *Pioneer Days*. . . . Other early successes showed him as an accomplished musician, dancer, etc., in *Opry House*, *Shindig*, *Birthday Party*, etc. . . .

Later Mickey's audience value improved when he began getting into difficulties and accomplishing things under pressure, as in *Barnyard Broadcast*. . . . Mickey can still be entertaining when things are running smoothly. . . .

Mickey is seldom funny in a chase picture, as his character and expressions are usually lost. . . . He is at his best when he sets out to do a thing with deadly determination despite annoyances and menace.

For the first two years of Mickey Mouse, Walt Disney and Ub Iwerks devoted their energies and talents to building their creation into a minor masterpiece. The equity of their partnership was signaled by the title card of *Steamboat Willie*:
"A Walt Disney Comic by Ub Iwerks."
Ub drew most of the first five Mickey cartoons, with the drawings in between the major moves supplied by Clark, Cannon, and Jackson. Ub also drew the first batch of Mickey Mouse comic strips, which King Features started distributing to

newspapers in January 1930. With the studio expanding, the Disneys hired a group of New York animators in the spring of 1929. Only then did others besides Ub begin drawing Mickey Mouse.

When Mickey Mouse was firmly established, Walt Disney began gazing at new horizons. It was a pattern that would dominate the rest of his career: having achieved one goal, he needed another, more challenging one. He never lost his concern and affection for the star who made him famous (Walt referred to him as "Mickey Mouse," whereas Donald was dismissed as "The Duck"). Periodically Walt would bring Mickey's career back from idleness and neglect with a prestigious new vehicle. And Walt was ever vigilant to preserve Mickey's character and dignity. When story men allowed their imaginations to overreach Mickey's capabilities, he cautioned them, "Remember, he's just a mouse."

ABOVE: Mickey's Nightmare (1932).

OPPOSITE: *Walt and his key coworkers stand behind a row of Mickeys in front of the Hyperion studio in 1930. Left to right: Dick Lundy, Tom Palmer, Johnny Cannon, Dave Hand, Bert Gillett, Wilfred Jackson, Bert Lewis, Walt Disney, Les Clark, Ben Sharpsteen, Norm Ferguson, Floyd Gottfredson, Jack King.*

CHAPTER TWO

ANIMATION BEFORE DISNEY

Early Attempts at Animation

From an eight-legged boar in the Altamira caves to Marcel Duchamp's *Nude Descending a Staircase*, human beings have always tried to capture movement in their art. Presumably, the artist in a cave in northern Spain thirty thousand years ago was dissatisfied with his drawing of a four-legged boar and added the extra legs to trick the eye into believing the animal was running. The critical reaction to his art is unknown, but Duchamp was excoriated when his painting of overlapping figures was displayed at the New York Armory Show in 1913.

A forerunner of today's comic strip can be found in an Egyptian wall decoration circa 2000 B.C. In successive panels it depicts two wrestlers struggling in a variety of holds. Illustrating proportions of the human figure, Leonardo da Vinci showed how the limbs would appear in various positions. Giotto's angels seem to take flight in his repetition of their movements. The Japanese used scrolls to tell a continuous story.

True animation could not be achieved until people understood a fundamental principle of the human eye: the persistence of vision. This was first demonstrated in 1828 by a Frenchman, Paul Roget, who invented the thaumatrope ("wheel of magic" in Greek). It was a disc with a string or peg attached to both sides. One side of the disc showed a bird, the other an empty cage. When the disc was twirled, the bird appeared in the cage. This proved that the eye retains images when it is exposed to a series of pictures, one at a time.

The thaumatrope was simply a visual trick. The phenakistoscope ("an optical deceiver" in Greek) achieved real animation. Invented by Joseph Plateau in 1826, it was a circular card with slits around the edge. The viewer held the card up to a mirror and peered through the slits as the card whirled. Through a series of drawings on the card, the eye perceived an acrobat doing flips or a horse performing tricks. Another important principle had been discovered; the spaces between the slits operated the way the shutter of a movie projector does today.

The same technique applied to the zoetrope ("burning life" in Greek). In 1860 Pierre Desvignes inserted a strip of paper containing drawings on the inside of a drumlike cylinder. The drum twirled on a spindle, and the viewer gazed through slots on the top of the drum. The figures in the drawing magically came to life, endlessly repeating an acrobatic feat.

PRECEDING SPREAD: *Newspaper cartoonist Winsor McCay infused his Gertie the Dinosaur with personality. Here Gertie encounters the woolly mammoth Jumbo* (SPREAD). *J. R. Bray spoofed the safari trips of Theodore Roosevelt in* Colonel Heeza Liar's African Hunt (INSET).

OPPOSITE: *In drawing proportions of the human figure, Leonardo da Vinci animated the arms and legs (circa 1492).*

TOP LEFT: *An eight-legged boar portrays movement in a prehistoric wall drawing in Spain.*

TOP: *The thaumatrope had a bird on one side of a disc and a cage on the other. Twirling the disc, the viewer perceived the bird in the cage.*

BELOW: *Wall decoration about 2000 B.C. shows how Egyptians made an attempt at animation.*

Again, the persistence of vision. Animation could be simulated as long as the eye had a brief pause between seeing the next picture in a sequence. The afterimage supplied the bridge to the next picture. The thaumatrope, phenakistoscope, and zoetrope provided entertainment in many a Victorian parlor.

In 1892, another Frenchman, Emile Reynaud, brought animation to show business. A painter of lantern slides, Reynaud was fascinated by the early attempts at animation. He improved on the zoetrope by replacing the slits with mirrors stuck side by side on the revolving center. The mirrors reflected the individual pictures on the inside of the drum, providing movement. He called his invention the praxinoscope.

He carried the idea further by drawing his pictures on black strips of paper. A separate card provided the background for the action drawings. The animation, which consisted of only twelve different poses, could be played against a variety of backgrounds.

Still Reynaud wasn't satisfied. Instead of the twelve poses on paper, he painted five hundred on hard, transparent gelatin. Small holes were punched in each picture, like the camera sprockets of today. The holes meshed into the teeth of a large wheel, rotating at the same speed as thirty-six mirrors in the center. Each picture was lighted individually, reflected on a mirror, and projected onto a screen. Reynaud's Théâtre Optique attracted a half-million Parisians between 1892 and 1900.

The kineograph was simply a flip book inside a large viewer. A series of progressive actions was drawn on successive pages. When the pages were riffled, the drawings seemed to move. The kineograph first appeared in 1868 and continues today in the form of children's toys and peepshows in penny arcades.

Animation in Motion Pictures

The development of the motion picture camera and projector by Thomas A. Edison and others provided the first really practical means of making drawings move. But the possibilities weren't explored until almost a decade after the movie industry was born. Three important figures were associated with the beginning of the animation industry: J. Stuart Blackton, Emile Cohl, and Winsor McCay.

Blackton was a young English-born adventurer who pioneered American films as one of the founders of Vitagraph in 1899. In 1906 he issued a short film *Humorous Phases of Funny Faces*. A sensation with audiences, the illusion was created by the simplest of means.

Comical faces were drawn on a blackboard, then erased. The camera was stopped after each face was photographed. The "stop-motion" provided a startling effect as the facial expressions changed before the audience's eyes. Blackton also experimented with animation in *The Haunted Hotel* (1906), *The Magic Fountain Pen* (1907), and other films.

Paris-born Emile Cohl was a political cartoonist who protested to the

Gaumont film company that it had stolen one of his cartoons for an ad. The Gaumont manager was impressed with the young man and gave him a job as gag man at the studio. In 1908 he made a two-minute film called *Phantasmagoria*, a work of rare imagination that required two thousand drawings. Movie audiences had already marveled at photographed objects moving on the screen; they were astounded to see drawings come to life. Cohl created all the drawings himself, as he did for one hundred other cartoons he made in France and the United States in the next ten years.

Working alone, Cohl produced crude art work, enlivened by his caricaturist talent. He created a little man, Fantoche, who is considered the first regular character to appear in animated films. Cohl anticipated the gags of later animators with hens that laid alarm clocks, obelisks that sighed, and a man who flew with his coat as a rudder.

Winsor McCay, dapper cartoonist for Hearst's New York *American*, was the first to apply showmanship to film animation. One day his son brought home something he had found in the rubble of a burned-out drugstore. It was a flip book to advertise a pharmaceutical firm. When McCay riffled the pages, he could see the action of the Bob Fitzsimmons-Jim Corbett heavyweight boxing match in 1897, the first championship fight on film.

McCay was fascinated. He turned the book over and on the blank pages drew pictures of his comic strip character, Little Nemo, in antic poses. Nemo moved! Using a stop-action camera, McCay produced his first cartoon film, *Little Nemo*, in 1908.

None of the three trailblazers of animation remained in the industry they helped to found. McCay, tired of multiple drawings, returned to newspaper cartooning. The innovative Blackton moved on to other kinds of filmmaking and died broke in 1941. Cohl went back to France before World War I and made no films after 1918. He died in utter poverty in 1938.

In 1909, Winsor McCay played vaudeville theaters with Gertie, the Trained Dinosaur, in a tour that awakened America to the magic of animation.

McCay appeared at the side of the stage in evening dress, carrying a whip. He introduced Gertie, an amiable dinosaur that appeared on the screen and did tricks more or less at her master's bidding. Gertie lifted her foot on cue, tossed a mammoth by the tail and danced to music.

Audiences were astonished. McCay wouldn't divulge his secrets, but his methods were simple. He carefully pinned a transparent sheet of paper on a drawing board with a 7-by-10-inch border outlined on it. Within this frame, he drew his action and background. The next piece of paper was placed over the first and the action varied slightly. The background was entirely retraced.

McCay repeated this process 960 times to achieve a minute on the screen. The painstaking McCay spent twenty-two months to make twenty-five-thousand drawings for The Sinking of the Lusitania, released in 1918.

ABOVE: Gertie the Dinosaur (1914) *was McCay's most outstanding achievement.*

TOP LEFT: *J. Stuart Blackton and one of his Funny Faces.*

The Industry Emerges in New York

"The early years of animation in New York were an exciting time," recalled Dick Huemer in 1957; he had started in 1916 and later became a Disney director. "The business attracted a strange breed—signpainters, salesmen, cartoonists—most of them failures. The rule was: if you could hold a pencil, you could animate.

"But we were a dedicated lot. We were pioneering a new industry, and having a vast amount of fun doing it. And money. As a kid I was making a hundred and fifty dollars a week. Some animators made four hundred dollars a week. Big money in those days." The New York animators buzzed with each innovation in the industry. J. R. Bray, a staff artist for the humor magazine Judge, produced The Dachshund and the Sausage in 1910, which is considered the first cartoon telling a story. The plot concerned a dog prevented by a pesky flea from eating a sausage. Bray also created Colonel Heeza Liar, a satire of the exploits of President Theodore Roosevelt, which became the first cartoon series.

Bray devised the practice of printing backgrounds on translucent sheets so the scenery would not need to be copied on every drawing. The characters were animated on these sheets; when a figure overlapped a background line, the line was scratched out.

Earl Hurd, who became a Disney story man in the Thirties, approached Bray in 1914 with the idea of tracing animation drawings in ink on celluloid sheets. The inked "cels" could be photographed against any background. The Bray-Hurd system became the standard practice in the industry.

Another pioneer, Bill Nolan, discovered the panorama or "pan" shot in 1913. Puzzled at how to show a figure skating against a small, framed background, he went to a drugstore and bought a roll of shelf paper. He drew a long scene on the paper. His figure remained stationary while the background scene was pulled past the camera, giving an illusion of speed.

Raoul Barré was a brilliant young artist who began animating in France, then moved his studio to New York and created Silas Bumpkin in the series The Grouch Chasers. Unlike other cartoon makers who worked in secrecy, Barré believed in letting

others know about his animation methods. He was the first to institute an apprentice system, a standard practice in cartoon studios today.

Barré's important contribution was the peg system. He punched holes at the top of the drawing paper. The holes were standard on the top of each sheet, fitting over pegs at the top of drawing boards and assuring an exact and rapid alignment of the drawings. Because the punched paper was heavier and not as transparent as previous paper, Barré devised the idea of drawing over a sheet of glass with a light under it.

Max Fleischer entered animation in 1917 with his ingenious *Out of the Inkwell*, in which the cartoon figure Koko the Clown interacted with Fleischer himself in live-action. Fleischer improved on the "rip and slash" technique first developed by Raoul Barré. The background of a scene would be drawn on one paper, the animated parts placed on top of the background. To reveal as much of the motionless parts as possible, pieces of the superimposed paper were cut away. The technique saved on animation costs and was widely used for a time. It was abandoned when Paul Terry introduced a complex method of laying cels on top of each other—one or more for the animated figures, one for background.

Absence of Personality

The new technologies helped the animation industry flourish during World War I and in the following years. Audiences were fascinated by the antics of the bizarre characters. The caliber of material didn't need to be high. Whenever stuck for a gag, an animator drew one character thumbing his nose at another. Like the flung custard pie in Mack Sennett comedies, it was always good for a laugh.

Most characters were devoid of personality, which is probably why none survived the advent of sound. The closest to achieving immortality was Felix the Cat by Pat Sullivan and Otto Messmer. He was a mischievous character who could survive a variety of scrapes, like Charlie Chaplin, but without being earthbound. His one great gimmick was pacing back and forth, deep in thought with hands behind his back, as he contemplated his next move.

*F*elix the Cat was the most popular star of silent cartoons. He was named Felix for "felicity"—a gesture toward improving the reputation of black cats. The Felix cartoons outshone competitors in the Twenties with their sophisticated humor and clever drawing. Like other silent stars, Felix was doomed by sound. His comedy was based on pantomime, and dialogue seemed out of place. The last regular Felix cartoon was released in August 1928, three months before the debut of Mickey Mouse. Several comebacks were attempted, including a television series, but Felix never recaptured his Twenties prominence.

Top: *Pat Sullivan drew the* Felix the Cat *comic strip as well as the animated cartoons.*

Above: *Felix the Cat's trademark was his pondering walk, which he could even perform on a tightrope.*

Many of the early cartoon characters were lifted intact from newspaper comics: John Foster's Katzenjammer Kids, *Jack King's* Happy Hooligan, *Raoul Barré's* Mutt and Jeff, *Leon Searl's* Krazy Kat *and Ignatz Mouse. Readers of the funny pages could recognize their favorites on the screen; they knew that Mutt was the guileless short fellow, and Jeff was the tall one who was always getting him in trouble.*

But the use of newspaper comic figures never proved successful in the long run. Many of them were not fully developed personalities in either medium. Many appeared in one-joke situations which became boring and predictable by repetition. All of them, especially the human characters, suffered in the transition to animation.

ABOVE: *The cinematic nature of comic strips such as* The Katzenjammer Kids *made them ideal for transference to movie cartoons.*

TOP RIGHT: *(From left to right) Horace Horsecollar, Clarabelle Cow, and Goofy make a merry threesome in this animation drawing.*

Paul Terry's Farmer Al Falfa was also a popular figure, but he was merely a human stooge amid a cast of animals. Most of the time he was the villain, and the story concerned the barnyard animals ganging up on him.

Animation of the human figure remained primitive. Audiences were amused by stylized animals cavorting on the screen. But there was something jarring about seeing a human in jerky, unrealistic movements. When animation became commercialized in the Twenties, little effort was made to improve drawing methods. The same tried-and-true systems prevailed: the Circle Formula and the Rubber-hose Method.

The quickest way to draw a character was to use circles, as Ub Iwerks did with Mickey Mouse. Round head, round eyes and nose, round body. The animator never had to worry about angles; no matter which way a character moved, he could be drawn with circular strokes.

Arms and legs moved like rubber hoses. No such things as elbows, knees, and wrists concerned the animator. Tubelike and rubbery limbs could be drawn fast and moved in any direction or elongated if necessary.

Speed and economy won out over reality. As long as characters were drawn with the Circle Formula, they would be as flat as those in the newspaper comic strips. There was no illusion of depth, as there was in live-action movies. The Rubber-hose Method further robbed the cartoon of realism.

The greatest handicap for conveying personality during the first two decades of the animation industry was the absence of sound. In today's cartoons, voice is the primary means of establishing character, and sound effects are a major tool for comedy. In silent films, dialogue was expressed in two ways: balloons above the characters' heads, as in comic strips; or full-screen titles. The first technique was totally unrealistic, the second interrupted the action.

Some animators tried to eliminate dialogue and tell their stories in pantomime, using crude facial expressions to indicate emotion. Not until Walt Disney and Ub Iwerks created Mickey Mouse did true personality appear in a cartoon. They were able to capitalize on sound for voices, sound effects and music. More importantly, Mickey was a dimensional character, bristling with gaiety and surprise, ever beguiling the audience. That was Disney's priceless contribution.

Storytelling in Early Cartoons

"Plots? We never bothered with plots. They were just a series of gags strung together. And not very funny, I'm afraid."

In 1957, Dick Huemer recalled his years of animating in New York cartoon studios before joining Disney.

"Usually there were three animators on a cartoon," said Huemer. "If we were working on a Mutt and Jeff cartoon, one of us might say, 'Let's make a picture about Hawaii.' Okay, fine. So each of us would work on a third of the picture. A couple of weeks later, we'd make a hookup. 'Where have you got 'em?' I'd ask. The other animator might have Mutt and Jeff on a surfboard at the end of his sequence. So I'd begin mine on a surfboard."

The gags were primitive and often based on violence, as is still true of cartoon shorts. One character would beat another mercilessly, only to have his victim instantly recover and return the favor. Perhaps the villain would swing a rapier and reduce the hero to baloney slices, which would be miraculously rejoined.

Anything could happen. An explosion would blow the features off a man's face, then he would pick them up and reassemble them. When Felix the Cat paced in a quandary, his tail detached to form a question mark over his head.

Albert Hurter and a few others strove to elevate the standards of animation. For a wartime Mutt and Jeff, Hurter drew a stunning display of an American flag flying over a captured German submarine. He made one series of forty drawings that were repeated and another of thirty drawings, also repeated. Ordinary animation would have depicted the flag in five to ten drawings, constantly repeated. Another artist, Dick Friel, created a beautiful water splash in forty or fifty frames instead of the usual eight.

But in the mid-Twenties, commercialism took over the animation industry. Big studios like International decreed to animators that a waving flag had to be accomplished with four or five drawings. A splash was depicted by four circles in the water. Animators were given quotas on the number of the drawings they had to produce each day. Cartoons had to be manufactured in quantity and cheaply, because theater owners would pay only small fees for "fillers" before the feature attraction.

The same gags were worked and reworked. Audiences became apathetic. The novelty of seeing cartoons move on the screen had long worn off.

The cartoon industry struck a depression. Studios shut down and animators were jobless. Many of the brilliant ones, discouraged by orders for speed and simplicity, departed for other fields of endeavor. The cartoonists who remained feared that the cartoon was doomed to an insignificant role on a movie bill.

"*Although anything was possible in the world of the cartoonist, we had to discover what we could do bit by bit,*" commented Ted Sears, another cartoon pioneer who became a Disney story man. "*The early artist didn't think of defying gravity. It was discovered by accident.*" Sears said that the man responsible was Albert Hurter, a Swiss-born artist whose drawings helped inspire Three Little Pigs, Snow White and the Seven Dwarfs, and Pinocchio. Hurter was animating an Alpine adventure of Mutt and Jeff. One scene showed Mutt leaning against a railing next to a precipice.

When the scene was photographed, the camera operator neglected to include the cel with the railing. The finished product showed Mutt leaning against thin air. Raoul Barré, a literal-minded Frenchman, was angry that a mistake had been made. But Hurter and the other artists laughed, realizing a new comedy device had been discovered.

The law of gravity was promptly repealed in every New York cartoon studio. Cartoon characters could walk on air, water, ceilings, clouds or sides of skyscrapers—and did.

TOP LEFT: *Sketches for Horace Horsecollar, Clarabelle Cow, and Clara Cluck illustrate the Circle and Rubber-hose techniques of animation.*

ABOVE: *Mutt and Jeff was another comic strip adapted to animation.*

CHAPTER THREE

DISNEY BEFORE MICKEY MOUSE

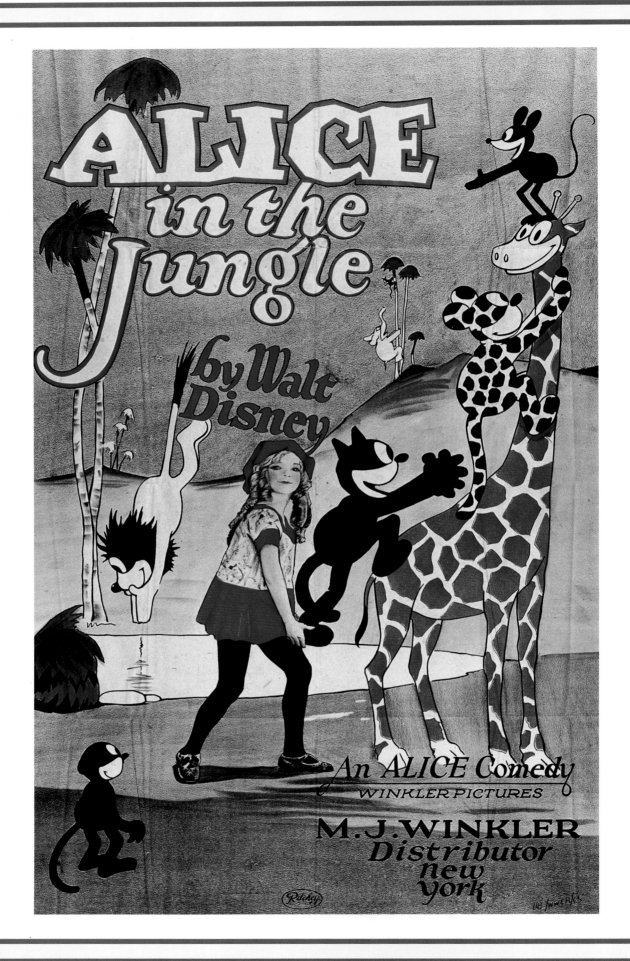

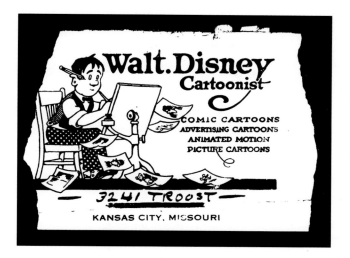

Kansas City and Laugh-o-Grams

"Everything is going fine with us and I am glad you made up your mind to come out. Boy, you will never regret it—this is the place for you—a real country to work and play in. . . . I can give you a job as artist-cartoonist and etc. with the Disney Productions, most of the work would be cartooning. Answer at once and let me know what you want to start. . . . At the present time I have one fellow helping me with animation and three girls doing the inking etc. while Roy handles the business end."

Walt Disney was writing from Los Angeles on June 1, 1924, to his good friend in Kansas City, Ub Iwerks. Walt and Roy had put up a sign Disney Brothers Studio on a small store at 4649 Kingswell Avenue and started producing Alice Comedies with the help of another animator, Rollin (Ham) Hamilton.

To fulfill his ambitious program, Walt needed help. He beseeched Ub to join him. Ub was a prodigious worker and a far better animator that Walt had ever been. Ub's arrival in California signaled the end of Walt's drawing career.

They had met in 1919 when both were seventeen and working for the Pesmen-Rubin Commercial Art Studio in Kansas City. Ub, born Ubbe Ert Iwwerks, was a Dutch immigrant's son, a high school dropout with a talent for lettering and airbrush work. Walt, born Walter Elias Disney in Chicago and reared on a Missouri farm and in Kansas City, had delivered mail, driven an ambulance in France after World War I, and turned to artwork against his father's wishes.

Laid off at Pesmen-Rubin after the Christmas season, Disney and Iwerks opened their own commercial art enterprise. Then Ub spotted an ad in the Kansas City *Star*:

Artist
Cartoon and Wash Drawings
First Class Man Wanted
Steady, Kansas City Slide Company
1015 Central

The two failed young entrepreneurs agreed that Walt should apply for the job. Walt was hired, and a month later he wangled a job for Ub. The company, which changed its name to Kansas City Film Ad, produced commercials that appeared in movie houses. Ub and Walt plunged into the world of animation.

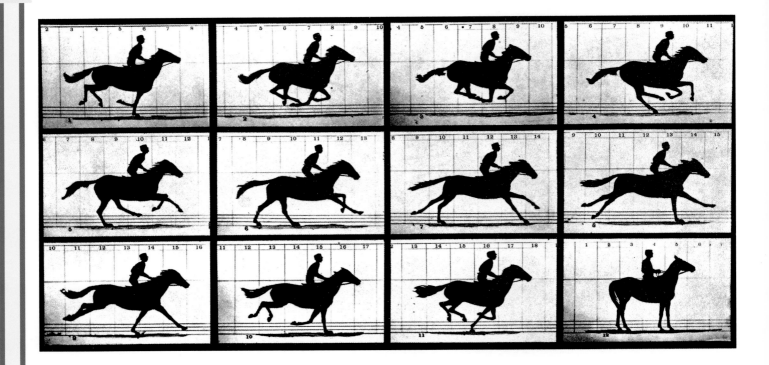

Dissatisfied with the primitive Film Ad animation, Walt wanted to know how the New York animators created their cartoons. At the public library he found a handbook by Carl Lutz and a book of Eadweard Muybridge's sequential photographs of animals and human figures in movement. He photostated the Muybridge photos, and he and Ub studied them to improve their drawing skills. Soon they were producing gag-filled cartoons for Film Ad.

TOP: Eadweard Muybridge made sequential photographs of a horse galloping, settling a bet that all four feet are off the ground at one time.

The methods were crude. Paper figures were cut out and pinned to sheets with background drawings. The figures were photographed on one frame of film, then moved slightly and photographed again. Walt prowled through all the departments, learning to operate the camera himself.

Walt moonlighted to produce Laugh-o-Grams, brief comic cartoons that appeared in three Kansas City theaters. They were successful enough to encourage Walt to incorporate Laugh-o-Gram Films in 1922. He convinced Ub to quit his job at Film Ad, and they hired five animators, most of them still in their teens. Laugh-o-Grams began making wry versions of *Little Red Riding Hood, Jack and the Beanstalk, Cinderella,* and other fairy tales.

President of his own company at 20 with a staff of ten, Walt Disney did some of the animation, operated the camera, and even washed the cels so they could be reused. To help keep the company solvent, he filmed news events for New York newsreel companies and took baby pictures for Kansas City parents. But such efforts were not enough, and Laugh-o-Grams was sliding into insolvency.

"We have just discovered something new and clever in animated cartoons!" Walt enthused in a letter to a New York distributor. He described his plan for a series of one-reelers in which child actors would intermingle with cartoon figures "not like *Out of the Inkwell* or Earl Hurd's, but of an entirely different nature."

The series would be called Alice Comedies.

The distributor encouraged Walt, and with his dwindling staff he embarked on his first short cartoon, *Alice's Wonderland.* Halfway through production, Walt ran completely out of funds. He described his plight to his older brother Roy, who was being treated for tuberculosis at a veterans' hospital in West Los Angeles. "Kid, I think you should get out of there," Roy counseled.

Disheartened, Walt decided to leave Kansas City. Laugh-o-Gram Films declared bankruptcy. By taking his camera door-to-door to photograph babies, he raised enough money to buy a one-way railroad ticket to California.

Young Man in Hollywood

After the Laugh-o-Grams fiasco, Walt Disney turned his back on animation. He had carted his camera and cartoon gear with him to California in 1923, but he kept the trunk locked. His ambition now was to become a motion picture director.

"No openings." Disney heard the same response at every studio. "Come back when you've had some experience."

The only experience he could acquire was riding a horse as an extra in a cavalry movie. His finances became precarious, and he had to borrow $5 from Roy to pay their Uncle Robert for board and room. Roy, who remained under treatment at the veterans' hospital, advised his brother, "I think you'd better give the cartoon business another try, Walt."

"No, I'm too late," said Walt. "I should have started six years ago. I don't see how I can top those New York boys."

Besides, there were no animators in Hollywood, and Walt realized his own shortcomings as an artist. He was confident in his skill at telling stories and devising gags, but he realized that Ub and the other animators at Laugh-o-Grams were better draftsmen. Eventually Walt had no choice except to unlock the trunk and

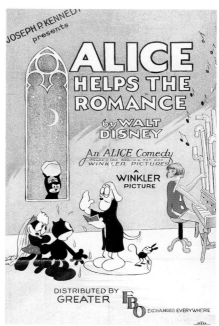

Alice's Wonderland continued to haunt Disney. He dispatched a letter to the distributor, Margaret Winkler, who had expressed interest in the series, telling her that he planned to embark on an ambitious program of Alice comedies. He convinced his Kansas City creditors to release the impounded film so she could view it. She responded favorably, offering $1,500 per negative.

"Let's go, Roy!" Walt exclaimed. "This is the break we have been waiting for."

The lifelong partnership began: Walt, the restless adventurer, ever seeking new goals of creativity; Roy, the steady hand, finding ways to realize his younger brother's dreams. Roy borrowed money to establish the Disney Brothers Studio, and production began on a new film, *Alice's Day at Sea.*

The bustling company of eight persons, including young new recruits from Kansas City, produced 56 Alice shorts before their modest popularity waned in 1927. The novelty of combining a real girl with cartoon figures had worn off, and new plots were hard to find. Disney's distributor, Charles Mintz, who had married Margaret Winkler and assumed control of her business, had become increasingly critical of the Alice cartoons. Carl Laemmle, the boss of Universal Pictures, told Mintz that he would like a cartoon series about a rabbit. Walt leaped to the idea and collaborated with Ub on rough pencil sketches of a proposed character.

"If these sketches are not what you want, let me know more about it, and I will try again," Walt wrote.

Ub and the staff hurriedly created the first of the Oswald the Lucky Rabbit cartoons, *Poor Papa,* in April 1927. Universal responded that the animation was jerky and repetitive, Oswald was dull and unfunny, and the story was merely a succession of gags. Walt stoutly defended Ub Iwerks, "whom I am willing to put alongside any man in the business today." He admitted that Oswald could be made "a younger character, peppy, alert, saucy and venturesome, keeping him also neat

In combining live action with cartoons, Walt first filmed Alice, played by young Virginia Davis, against a white backdrop. Then he and Ham Hamilton made drawings to augment the action and reexposed the negative, frame by frame. After completing six Alice comedies, Walt felt secure enough to send for Ub Iwerks.

TOP LEFT: *The animals give Alice a welcoming parade in her first cartoon, Alice's Wonderland, 1923.*

TOP: *Disney made fifty-seven Alice comedies from 1923 to 1927. The first Alice was Virginia Davis, seen here in the sixth of the series,* Alice and the Dog Catcher.

ABOVE: *Left to right: Friz Freleng, Walker Harman, Walt Disney, Margie Gay, Rudolf Ising, Ub Iwerks, Hugh Harman, Roy Disney.*

and trim." But an excess of plot in a one-reeler would eliminate the funny stuff, he warned.

Walt and Ub worked long hours to inject more appeal into Oswald. Slowly the rabbit evolved into a rounder, softer, more accessible character. Unlike the New York cartoon studios that employed every cost-cutting method possible, Walt refused to stint on quality. He didn't allow his animators to use cycles—repeating the same action over and over to save production time. Rough animation was photographed and reviewed in a makeshift projection room—the origin of the "sweatbox," as it is still called. If the rough animation did not meet Walt's standards, it was returned to the animator for improvement.

Such attention to quality added to production costs—and Roy's headaches—but it paid off at the box office. Oswald the Lucky Rabbit cartoons attracted warm reviews in the trade press, and even the New York animators began marveling at the ingenious cartoons from the West Coast. The Disney brothers, who had moved into a new studio on Hyperion Avenue near Mack Sennett's comedy factory, added to the staff and began producing Oswald cartoons every two weeks.

The future seemed unlimited—until Walt journeyed to New York to renegotiate the contract with Mintz. Then the bombshell: Oswald had been snatched away, along with most of Walt's animators. In his eagerness to sell Oswald, Disney had failed to notice that Universal owned the copyright. "Never again will I work for somebody else," Disney vowed to his wife Lilly. Enter Mickey Mouse.

Exit Ub Iwerks

The avalanche of acclaim in the world's theaters and press for Mickey Mouse produced one casualty: Ub Iwerks.

Perhaps it was inevitable, despite the mutual bond of the two young animators who had risen from the Pesmen-Rubin Studio to preeminence in the cartoon world. Both were similarly ego-driven men, though Walt was more outgoing and Ub withdrawn. Walt was a showman, a born actor and a visionary. Ub was the hard-striving artist, unmatched in his fluid style as well as his volume of output. Walt was Irish and quick-tempered. Ub was Dutch and stubborn. He watched with growing discontent as Disney won world recognition as the father of Mickey Mouse, while little attention was paid to the artist who had given Mickey form and movement.

Friction between the two partners surfaced in 1929, when Ub was animating most of the Mickey Mouse cartoons. Disney made a practice of returning to the studio at night to take care of business matters and review Ub's drawings. Walt often created his own exposure sheets (the form detailing the action, dialogue and music, frame by frame), causing Ub to complain the next day, "That's not the way I planned it." He discarded Walt's sheets and made his own. After several complaints, Walt agreed not to interfere.

Disagreement between the two creative partners continued. Ub believed that his drawing of Mickey played the key role in the series' success, and he was jealous of any encroachment on his domain. Walt's concern for Mickey was intensely proprietary; he had learned from the Oswald experience to retain complete control of his enterprise.

In January 1930, Ub Iwerks announced he had accepted an offer to create a cartoon series of his own. He was leaving the Disney studio.

"I can't believe it," said the astonished Walt. He and Ub had worked side-by-side all day and into the night for the better part of eight years. They had spent more

TOP LEFT: *Alice (Margie Gay) faces the firing squad.*

ABOVE: *The beginnings of the Disney studio on Hyperion Avenue.*

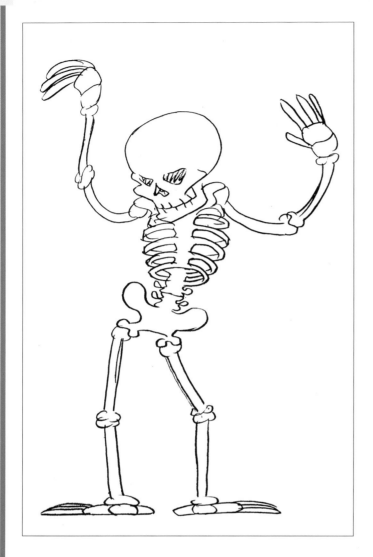

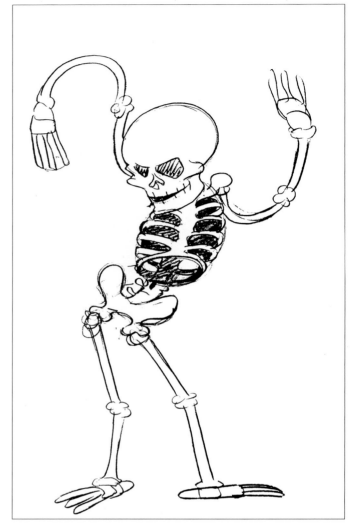

time together than they had with their wives. Walt was hurt, as well as apprehensive because the studio was losing its most gifted animator.

Ub could not be dissuaded. He relinquished his 20 percent interest in the Disney company for $2,920 and opened the Ub Iwerks studio in Hollywood. He launched a series called Flip the Frog. While technically proficient, the series lacked the personality and storytelling that Walt had injected into Alice, Oswald and Mickey Mouse. MGM released Flip the Frog, but it faded after thirty-seven episodes. Ub invented another series about a boy, Willie Whopper, but it failed to catch on.

For ten years Walt Disney and Ub Iwerks maintained an icy relationship. Then in 1940, Ben Sharpsteen convinced the two old friends to reconcile. Ub had tired of trying to maintain his enterprise in the fiercely competitive Hollywood; he wanted to pursue his real passion: developing technical processes. Walt welcomed him back to the studio. Both were undemonstrative, but their fellow workers recognized the deep bond between the two men.

Ub Iwerks became a valuable member of the Disney company. He designed the first multihead optical printer that facilitated the combining of animation and live action. He continued developing new techniques and devices for Disney and Disneyland until his death in 1971.

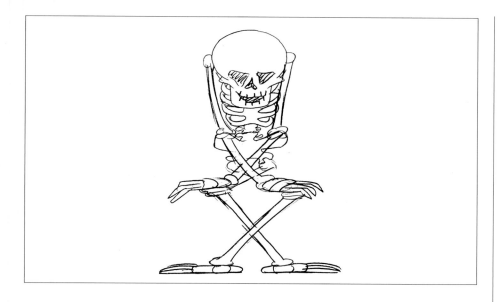

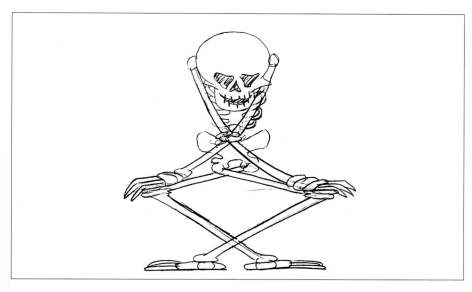

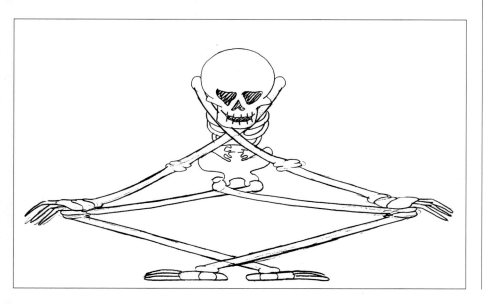

Disney was determined his studio not be overwhelmed by one character, as had happened with Alice and Oswald. He welcomed the suggestion of Carl Stalling, the studio's music director, for a series of shorts based on musical compositions. Stalling's first idea was a graveyard frolic to the music of Grieg's March of the Dwarfs.

Both Disney and Iwerks sparked to the idea. They devised a series of gags with skeletons floating out of graves and cavorting in a loose-boned chorus dance that even incorporated some of the Black Bottom and Charleston dance steps of the Twenties. There was no story, just one ghostly scene after another.

Iwerks plunged into the animation of The Skeleton Dance with the same demonic fervor he had given to Steamboat Willie. "I am glad the spook dance is progressing so nicely—give her Hell, Ubbe," Walt wrote from New York. "Make it funny, and I am sure we will be able to place it in a good way."

Disney masked his discontent with Ub's intransigence. Although Les Clark animated the opening scene, Iwerks insisted on drawing every remaining frame, allowing assistants only to fill in details. Disney disliked having his best animator tied up, but his arguments made no headway with the inflexible Ub, who felt he could achieve a flow of action only if he drew every scene himself.

Disney's distributor viewed The Skeleton Dance and complained, "They don't want this. MORE MICE." A theater manager termed it "too gruesome." But the public was charmed, and Disney was encouraged to launch a new series called Silly Symphonies.

CHAPTER FOUR
PREPARING FOR GREATNESS

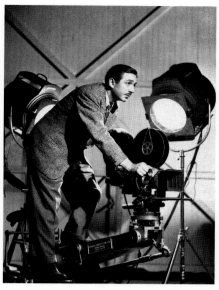

Color Comes to Animation

To achieve what he envisioned for animation, Walt Disney needed color, lots of it. He had instructed his technicians to experiment with nitrates and other solutions that might provide color on film, but nothing worked. The only thing possible was the tinting that had been done since the earliest movies—blue could be used for a night scene, red for a big fire. Early attempts had been made at hand-tinting details of the actual film, but that proved laborious and impractical.

During the Twenties, Technicolor developed a two-color process that was used successfully in films like Douglas Fairbanks's *The Black Pirate* in 1926. But the process was expensive and failed to provide true color, so producers lost interest in it. Then in 1932, Technicolor devised a method of combining the primary colors on three strips of negative. The process would not be ready for live-action movies until 1935, when *Becky Sharp* was released. But the process was suitable for cartoons.

"That was what we'd been waiting for," Walt recalled later. "When I saw those three colors all on one film, I wanted to cheer."

Roy Disney was not as enthusiastic. The company had just entered into a distribution deal with United Artists, said Roy, warning that United Artists would not advance more money for color.

Walt argued that the excitement of color would bring longer playdates for Disney cartoons and hence return more money to the company. When his brother expressed concern that colors might not stick to the celluloid or would chip off, Walt replied, "Then we'll develop paints that *will* stick and *won't* chip." He added that color would help popularize the Silly Symphonies, which had never matched the bookings achieved by Mickey Mouse.

As often happened, Walt prevailed. He insisted on strict terms with Technicolor: Disney would have a two-year exclusive which would prohibit other cartoon makers from using the three-color process.

Flowers and Trees *opens with the woodland animals enjoying the delights of spring. The camera switches quickly to the bright figures of an orange centipede, yellow daisies, and tan mushrooms.*

The hero and heroine are introduced. Both are trees, she a demure sapling with a yellow trunk, a light green clump of hair, and dark green fans on her arms; he with a dark brown thatch and a light brown trunk. The villain is a nasty gray stump with a green tongue. Spurned by the heroine, the villain rubs twigs together, Boy Scout style, and tosses flames in her direction. Bright red and yellow flames dance everywhere, threatening trees, birds, flowers, and mushrooms alike. The birds save the day by divebombing white clouds that spray out the fire. The hero and heroine are wed and clinch against a bright rainbow.

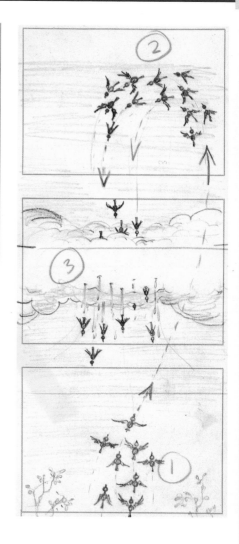

Disney called a halt to a new Silly Symphony called *Flowers and Trees*, which was halfway through animation. The backgrounds were repainted with color, and so was the action. The studio was pioneering all the way. Disney artists had applied color to cels to give more tone to the black-and-white shorts, but its extensive use had never been attempted.

"The colors were basic," commented Wilfred Jackson, one of the earliest Disney employees. "We had no choice in those days. Later we had our own standard paint mixes at the studio. But then we had to use commercial poster paint or whatever we could find. Some of it faded, some fell off the celluloid. We had to feel our way along."

Some studio artists favored muting the colors and attempting subtle shades. "We're paying a lot for color," Walt decreed. "Let's use it."

Jackson remarked, "Walt was right. In those days, there hadn't been many pictures in color. Audiences were impressed by the bright reds and greens and yellows. After color pictures became more common, we could afford to be more subtle."

By today's standards, the coloring of *Flowers and Trees* is far from subtle. But its release brought fresh praise for Walt Disney's inventiveness, as well as the extended bookings that Walt had predicted to Roy. The Academy of Motion Picture Arts and Sciences, honoring the cartoon medium for the first time, gave the Oscar to *Flowers and Trees* for best cartoon short of 1932.

Color brought a new dimension to cartoons, but also new problems. Before color, it was simple to make characters legible; they were outlined in black against a light background. Color required close coordination so animated figures would "read well" against backgrounds.

A red character against a purple background would be disturbing to the eye. A green figure standing before a green tree would disappear into the foliage. The issue was often solved by keeping the characters in lively colors and graying out the backgrounds.

"Look out the window and you will see there is gray in everything—the trees, the sky, the mountains," pointed out veteran Disney color-stylist Art Riley. "By painting our backgrounds with overtones of gray, we can make the scenes look natural and allow the animated figures to be legible." Gray need not be a somber color. Warmth can be found in gray-violets and gray-greens.

"Absorbing color is like eating a steak. The first few bites seem wonderful. But too much steak can make you tired of it. So can too much color."

OPPOSITE TOP: *The vivid hues of nature proved ideal for Disney's burst into color.*

OPPOSITE BOTTOM AND TOP LEFT: *Story sketch pages for* Flowers and Trees.

ABOVE: *The story artist captures the movement of birds in flight.*

Scene I
first pig building straw house.

Scene II Second pig building house of sticks.

Scene III Third pig building house of brick.

ABOVE: *Story sketches show the differing houses of the Three Little Pigs.*

TOP RIGHT: *Artist's concept of the Wolf's comeuppance.*

Triumph of Character: *Three Little Pigs*

Walt Disney, who enjoyed showing off his cartoon domain to famous visitors, was escorting Mary Pickford through the studio one day in 1932. "America's Sweetheart" adored Mickey Mouse, and she listened raptly as Walt explained the process of creating a Mickey cartoon.

The party stopped at an office where a new Silly Symphony was being planned. On the walls were drawings of three pudgy little pigs and a terrifying wolf.

Walt had started preliminary work on *Three Little Pigs* a few months before. Albert Hurter created charming sketches of the characters, and a story was being developed. Walt argued that the short needed an added value, perhaps a jingle to help tell the story. Frank Churchill, a Disney musician, picked out a tune on the piano. Ted Sears, the story man, contributed couplets that helped tell the story. The chorus fell into place: "Who's afraid of the big bad wolf?" They couldn't think of an ending to the chorus until Pinto Colvig, the voice of numerous cartoon characters, suggested a few bars on a fiddle or fife.

"Why don't you do that 'pig' thing for Mary?" Walt suggested.

With Churchill on the piano, Sears with a fiddle, and Colvig playing an ocarina, the song was performed for the famous visitor. "If you don't make this cartoon about the pigs," Miss Pickford threatened Walt, "I'll never speak to you again."

Disney had already been convinced of the possibilities of *Three Little Pigs*, especially during a time when millions of Americans were "trying to keep the wolf from the door." He assigned Dick Lundy and Fred Moore to animate the pigs, Norm

Ferguson for the wolf. Bert Gillett was the director, but Disney oversaw every phase of the production. In a memo, he exhorted his staff to contribute more comedy for the cartoon:

> . . . . The building of the houses holds chances for a lot of good gags. All this action would be set within rhythm and should work out very effectively. . . . Pull quite a few gags of the wolf trying to get into the little houses, and the pigs' attempts to get rid of him. Chances for funny ways in which the little pigs attack him, the different household props they would use. . . . The idea of the pigs having musical instruments gives us a chance to work in the singing and dancing angles for the finish of the picture. . . . Might try to stress the angle of the little pig who worked the hardest, received the reward, or some little story that would teach a moral. . . .
>
> All gags must be handed in by Friday afternoon December 30 at 4 P.M. I expect a big turnout on this story in spite of Christmas.

Production moved swiftly, and Walt delivered Three Little Pigs to the New York distributors. "How come you give us a cartoon with only four characters?" one of them demanded. "We got our money's worth with [the April 1933 Silly Symphony] Father Noah's Ark."

Disney shrugged off the comment. He knew from Los Angeles previews that he had a hit. He wrote to his brother Roy: "At last we have achieved true personality in a whole picture."

Released in May 1933 at the depth of the Depression, Three Little Pigs was acclaimed by the nation. The wolf was on many American doorsteps, and "Who's Afraid of the Big Bad Wolf?" became a rallying cry. Theaters billed the cartoon over the feature attraction, and many kept it week after week as the rest of the bills changed.

The plot was simplicity itself. The two frivolous pigs would rather sing and play than build suitable shelter against the evil wolf. The industrious pig constructs a wolf-resistant brick house. The wolf arrives and blows away the straw and twig

Top: *The sketch illustrates the stealthy approach of the Wolf.*

Above: *Disney listens with satisfaction to the voices of the Three Little Pigs (Pinto Colvig, Mary Moder, Dorothy Compton) singing "Who's Afraid of the Big Bad Wolf?" Composer Frank Churchill on piano.*

Below: *Animation drawing of the straw-building Pig.*

ADD MENACE PROPS

WOLF PACIFIER

houses of the two silly pigs. They rush to the house of their serious-minded brother. The wolf is foiled, falls into a boiling kettle, and flees. The pigs celebrate with a song.

Some of the picture is crude. As a hangover from silent days, exclamation marks appear when the pigs are terrified and when the wolf slaps his hands, pretending to walk away.

But it is easy to see why *Three Little Pigs* proved a sensation. It is full of clever uses of sound and color. Mortar makes a juicy sound when slapped on brick. The pursuing wolf is crowned with a treeful of red apples and then a rotten brown one. His face turns blue, then purple as his huffing and puffing fails against the brick house. Character is the element that makes *Three Little Pigs* great. The first pig plays his flute to a gay song and kicks his feet nimbly. The second pig shows his flighty nature as he fiddles and jigs. They sing in boyish falsettos. The builder pig talks his songs in businesslike tones and works with sharp, deliberate motions. He is in overalls, not the sailor suits of his brothers.

The wolf is a shaggy, stealthy villain who slinks from tree to tree with an evil eye. He drools at the prospect of succulent porkers for dinner and concocts cunning schemes to snare them. The ending is perfect: the triumph of good over evil and industry over sloth.

Character, plot, and songs combined in 8 1/2 minutes of rare entertainment. The distributors clamored: "Send us more pigs." Walt, who detested repeating himself, refused, but Roy convinced him to try three more: *The Big Bad Wolf, Three Little Wolves,* and *The Practical Pig.* None approached the success of the first picture. Walt often commented in the years to follow: "You can't top pigs with pigs."

Disney reluctantly brought back his new villain to menace Little Red Riding Hood in **The Big Bad Wolf** (LEFT). He also appeared in **Three Little Wolves** (OPPOSITE AND TOP). Except for a wartime government film, the Wolf's theatrical career was over.

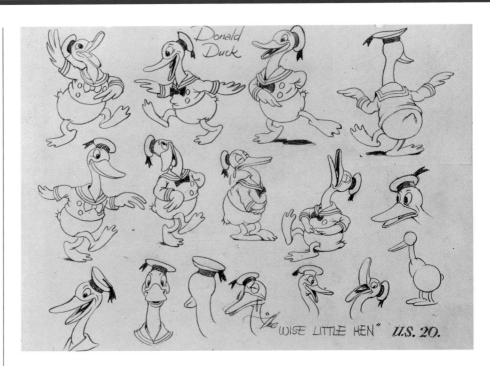

Donald's character was outlined in a 1939 interstudio memo by a story man:

The Duck is the most versatile of all the Disney characters, He can carry off any role with honors—except dumb roles or gentleman parts. . . . He is vain, cocky and boastful, loves to impose on other people and heckle them; but if the tables are turned, he flies into a rage. . . . It is his cockiness that gets him into most of his scrapes, because it is seasoned with foolhardy recklessness. . . . His most likable trait is determination. . . . The Duck never compromises. Regardless of the odds against him, he comes back again and again into the fray.

When attacking a problem, he may be either cocky, cautious or cunning—or all three by turns. He seldom flies into a rage at his first rebuffs; usually those defeats serve to bring out his cleverness.

He doesn't stay angry for long periods; even in his wildest rages, he can be completely and instantly mollified with a little gratification. . . . He is easily amused and laughs especially heartily when he thinks he has caused some person or thing discomfort.

TOP RIGHT: *Character sketches for Donald's debut, before the metamorphosis.*

The Advent of Donald Duck

"Who—me? Oh, no! I got a bellyache."

These were the opening lines for the debut of Donald Duck in *The Wise Little Hen*, a 1934 Silly Symphony. He was a supporting player, a long-beaked bird in sailor's cap and jacket, four feathers for hands and spiky tailfeathers.

He is first seen doing a sailor's hornpipe aboard a boat as the hen and her chicks seek help in planting corn. The duck feigns a stomach ailment to avoid work. He and lazy Peter Pig retire to the Idle Hour Club. They end up kicking each other when they are not invited to a luscious corn dinner prepared by the hen.

It was an inauspicious beginning, but clearly the duck had possibilities. They were realized in his next cartoon, *Orphan's Benefit*. Prophetically, he stole the picture from Mickey Mouse.

Mickey calls on Donald to help entertain the orphans. Donald insists on reciting "Mary Had a Little Lamb" and "Little Boy Blue" in his sputtering, half-understandable voice despite the jeers of his youthful audience. When the vegetables start flying, Donald explodes in a Vesuvian tantrum.

Audiences were convulsed by the foolish, bad-tempered bird, and he became a regular cast member in the Mickey Mouse series. He played a peace officer in *The Dognapper*, a peanut vendor in *Mickey's Band Concert*, a fireman in *Mickey's Fire Brigade*. Between 1935 and 1942, Donald costarred in twenty-six Mickey Mouse cartoons. In 1937 he became the second Disney character to star in his own series, portraying a Latin lover in *Don Donald*.

Donald Duck was first drawn by Dick Lundy. Jack Hannah, who later directed the cartoons, once said of Donald, "I could kill him sometimes. But he can be fun to work with."

The main limitation of Donald, said Hannah, was the voice (squawked by Clarence Nash). The words could not be understood by many in the audience. But the voice was so comical and fit Donald's explosive nature so neatly that other

TOP: *By the time of his sixth cartoon, Mickey's Fire Brigade (1935), Donald Duck had become a major player (animation drawing).*

LEFT: *In Orphan's Benefit (1941), Donald reprised the role that helped make him famous.*

ABOVE: *Story sketch for Don Donald (1937), the duck's first starring role.*

ABOVE: *Story sketch for* Don Donald.

BELOW: *Animation of Donald in* The Wise Little Hen *caught his infectious jauntiness.*

storytelling devices were used: the dialogue was repeated by another character with a clear voice, or the plot was related in pantomime. Most of the payoff gags in Donald Duck cartoons featured action, not dialogue.

Donald's appearance changed after his debut. The long bill was shortened to a more expressive size. His angular figure was rounded to make him cuter and more maneuverable.

Donald Duck's versatility is demonstrated by the fact that he has appeared in four feature films, more than any other Disney character including Mickey Mouse. He also works better than the others when appearing with live actors; he doesn't seem out of place, as some of the other characters do. For instance, he frequently exchanged dialogue with Walt Disney on the *Disneyland* television show.

Over the years Donald Duck has enjoyed a steadier career than Mickey Mouse, whom he replaced as the studio's number-one comedy star. Mickey suffered an eclipse in the late Thirties. He had started his career as something of a scamp, but public pressure had softened his character, made him more of a leading actor than a comic. Animators were more comfortable with the easy comedics of Donald, Goofy, and Pluto, who had animal-like proportions. "What can you do with a four-foot mouse?" the artists pondered. Mickey also suffered from a lack of attention from his mentor. Walt Disney had loftier goals than dreaming up gags for Mickey Mouse.

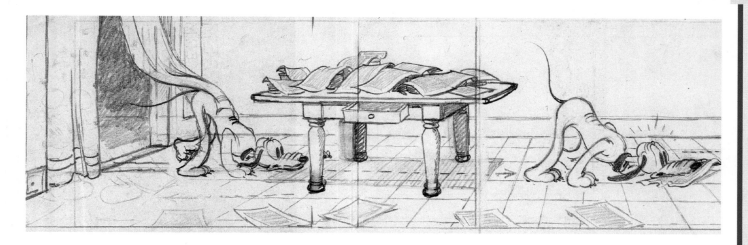

New Stars for the Disney Roster

Pluto made his debut in a brother act in *The Chain Gang*, a 1930 Mickey Mouse. He was one of a pair of bloodhounds chasing Mickey after an escape from a prison. What made Pluto's debut memorable was a closeup, something relatively novel in cartoons. The dog raced up to the camera, his panting mouth almost filling the screen. Audiences were startled and amazed.

Like the late Peter Pig, one of the hounds disappeared, but his partner showed up in another cartoon with Mickey Mouse, *The Picnic*. This time he was given a name, Rover. He threw the whole picnic into an uproar when he rampaged in pursuit of a rabbit while being tethered to Mickey's car.

Rover was so successful that Disney decided he could be a permanent foil for Mickey. But he needed a better name. Pal and Homer the Hound were proposed. Disney suggested Pluto, and the name stuck.

In his next film, *The Moose Hunt*, Pluto spoke. The event was not as auspicious as Greta Garbo's first words in a talkie. In the scene Mickey believes mistakenly that he will be forced to shoot his pet dog, and he pleads, "Speak to me!" Mickey is astonished when Pluto replies, "Kiss Me!"

The line brought a big laugh, but it was out of character.

"We've generally kept Pluto all dog," explained Nick Nichols, longtime animator of Pluto. "He usually keeps all four paws on the ground, and he doesn't speak, except for a breathy 'Yeah! Yeah!' and a panting, raspy kind of laugh. When he talks to other animals, he uses what I call garbage—a combination of growls, gurps and mutters."

His only other venture into dialogue came in *Mickey's Pal Pluto*, in which his good and evil selves debate his actions.

Walt Disney won an Academy Award in 1941 for the Pluto cartoon *Lend a Paw*, the studio's sixth Oscar in six years. Animators have nominated Pluto for another award: being the first cartoon character to break away from the old style of animation. He was not a flat figure that had been obviously drawn. He seemed as round and plump as an oversized sausage. He owed nothing to the Circle Formula or the Rubber-hose Method. He had his own size and shape, and he moved convincingly.

He could also reason, which may seem like a minor matter, but its value was overlooked for a long time. Early cartoon characters could think in elementary

TOP AND ABOVE: *Story sketches for* Playful Pluto, *in which he displays reasoning powers.*

BELOW: *Finished animation of Pluto in* Lend a Paw.

ABOVE AND BELOW: *Animation drawings of Goofy dancing with a mop in* Mickey's Birthday Party *(1942)*.

TOP RIGHT AND OPPOSITE TOP: *Story sketches of the cake catastrophe for* Mickey's Birthday Party.

O.S. EXCLAMATIONS
GOOF BOWS

terms: a bright notion was symbolized by an electric light over the head. But these pioneering figures had little reasoning power; they merely reacted to outside forces. Only when cartoon characters learned to reason could they be entirely convincing.

The classic example of Pluto's reasoning was the flypaper sequence in the 1934 *Playful Pluto*, animated by the gifted Norm Ferguson. Sniffing along in his usual style, Pluto encounters a sheet of flypaper. His nose sticks to it. He figures he can get rid of the flypaper by holding it with his paw. Now his paw is stuck. He continues taking step after logical step, only to become further entrapped by the sticky paper.

Here is an analysis of Pluto's character, prepared as a guide for story men, animators, and comic-book artists:

"Pluto is best appreciated when he is not too smart. . . . In pantomime, his dumb, one-track mind is similar to that of Stan Laurel's. . . . Pluto is nervous and sensitive, easily startled. . . . His feelings are easily hurt when scolded, especially by Mickey. . . .

"He is foolhardy rather than brave. He might be termed a likable coward. . . . His loyalty to Mickey is a good asset. . . . Pluto will bark at anything strange, but he will retreat hastily when it makes a move toward him. . . . His natural facial expression, when not happy or angry, is sad and mournful."

Unlike Pluto, Goofy was a dog who spoke, though in a halfwitted gurgle, and assumed human proportions and costumes. Goofy's debut came in 1932 with *Mickey's Revue*. He was simply the member of an animal audience watching a musical show. Wearing pince-nez glasses and whiskers, he munched on peanuts and laughed. But what a laugh! It was deep-throated and convulsive, as delivered by the former circus clown Pinto Colvig.

Goofy evolved slowly. At first he was named Dippy Dawg, and he provided minor comic relief in such shorts as *The Whoopee Party*, *Touchdown Mickey*, and *The Klondike Kid*. He began as a genuine hayseed, the kind that Disney had known on his

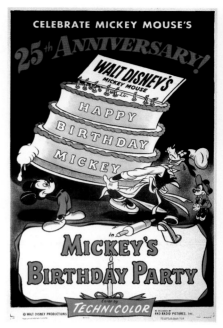

THROWS CAKE O.S.

BELOW: *Animation drawing of Mickey getting the worst of it, thanks to Goofy, in* Mickey's Fire Brigade *(1935).*

boyhood farm in Marceline, Missouri. Then he became a likable bucktoothed dolt, slow on the uptake but willing to go along with the schemes of Mickey and Donald. The tall lumpy hat remained, but the white vest was exchanged for a rumpled suit or overalls.

Art Babbitt is credited with elevating Goofy from bit player to star. The animator gave him a pattern of mannerisms and a loony, flat-footed shuffle similar to the walk assumed by black comedians. In a 1934 memo, Babbitt analyzed his protégé:

"Think of the Goof as a composite of an everlasting optimist, a gullible Good Samaritan, a halfwit, a shiftless, good-natured hick. He is loose-jointed and gangly, but not rubbery. He can move fast if he has to, but would rather avoid overexertion so he takes what seems the easiest way. . . .

"He very seldom, if ever, reaches his objective or completes what he has started. . . . Any little distraction can throw him off his train of thought. . . . His brain being rather vapory, it is difficult for him to concentrate on any one subject.

"Yet the Goof is not the type of halfwit that is to be pitied. He doesn't drool, dribble or shriek. He is a good-natured dumbbell who thinks he is pretty smart."

Through the Thirties Goofy proved an ideal scene-stealing foil for Mickey and Donald. Finally in 1939 he achieved star status in *Goofy and Wilbur*, a fishing adventure with a friendly grasshopper. On his own, Goofy became far more versatile, even though his lines were reduced to little more than the trade-mark laugh, yelps of pain and terror and the bashful "Gawrsh!"

Jack Kinney introduced a whole new career for Goofy with *How to Ride a Horse* in 1941. Kinney devised a formula in which a serious, slightly pompous voice (sketch artist John McLeish) narrated the various steps in learning to ride horseback. Goofy with mock concentration demonstrated the steps, always falling into comical predicaments. The juxtaposition of the straightarrow narrator and the terminally maladroit Goof was pure magic, and the How To series continued into the mid-Fifties, when the making of cartoon shorts came to a halt.

ABOVE AND OPPOSITE TOP: *Minnie in Mickey's Rival (1936).*

RIGHT: *Story sketch of the two sweethearts in Mickey's Rival.*

BELOW: *The mail brings portent of trouble in Donald's Nephews (1938).*

OPPOSITE BOTTOM: *A story sketch of Daisy Duck in her 1937 film debut, Don Donald (LEFT). In the same film, she dances the fandango while Donald plays guitar (RIGHT).*

Leading Ladies and Supporting Players

From *Steamboat Willie* onward, Disney required leading ladies, hence the presence of Minnie Mouse, Daisy Duck, and—for Pluto—Fifi the Peke and Dinah the Dachshund. They were necessary as objects to be wooed or rescued. But none of the female characters ever emerged as more than faintly defined ingenues. The cartoons were comedies, and audiences were less apt to laugh at the indignities that befell female figures (exception: Betty Boop). The fact that all the animators were male may have been a factor.

Minnie appeared in seventy of the 129 Mickey Mouse cartoons, often in brief roles, and in none of the feature films, except for a token appearance in *Who Framed Roger Rabbit*. Only in a few cartoons, such as *Mickey's Rival* and *The Nifty Nineties*, does she have a substantial part.

In the 1938 *Donald's Nephews*, Donald Duck receives a postcard from his sister Dumbella that she was sending her three "angel children" for a visit. Donald's delight turns to rage when Huey, Dewey, and Louie wreak havoc on the house with a wild polo match on tricycles. The nephews immediately became the perfect instigation for Donald's tantrums, and they appeared in twenty-four of the Donald Duck cartoons.

Two more nemeses for Donald were introduced in 1943 with *Private Pluto*. These were pesky chipmunks who were given names in their third cartoon: Chip an' Dale. With their round furry bodies, wide cheeks, and prominent teeth, they became popular enough to star in their own series.

A few early Disney characters faded from the scene. Clarabelle Cow and

Pegleg Pete was a superb heavy who predated Mickey Mouse, having appeared in both the Alice and Oswald cartoons. A combination of Wallace Beery and an alley cat (though he sometimes resembled a ferocious dog), Pete provided the first menace for Mickey Mouse, twisting Mickey's body like chewing gum in Steamboat Willie. *He served as a Mexican bandit, French trapper, evicting sheriff, bullying train conductor, always being trounced in the end by Mickey or Donald. Whenever a first-class villain was required, Pete was pressed into service, right up to 1990 in* The Prince and the Pauper.

Horace Horsecollar were engaging figures in the early Thirties cartoons, and they combined well together. Their pipestem legs and grotesque faces harked back to the Rubber-hose style of animation, and they were phased out in favor of more realistic characters.

The Animators Go to School

Except for a few studio-trained artists, most of the animators at Disney were self-taught cartoonists from the New York school. They brought zest and exhilaration to the Disney pictures, but their methods were the same that cartoonists had employed since the beginning of the medium.

Disney once remarked: "A lot of the artists who came to me from the East and had been in the business a good number of years were individualists. They insisted they not only draw, but they wanted to do the inking. They wanted to follow it to the last detail. I said, 'That's silly. You draw it and then we have people who can do the inking better than you can.' I had quite a time breaking that down."

Early in the studio's history, Disney concluded that he needed a new and different breed of animator to realize his plans for the future. He couldn't afford to start a school of his own, so in 1931 he arranged for his artists to attend classes at the Chouinard Art Institute in downtown Los Angeles. The studio paid the tuition. Many of the young men did not own cars, so Walt drove them to Chouinard. He returned to the studio for an evening's work, then drove back to the school and distributed the students to their homes.

"To do the things I wanted to do, I needed better artists," Disney told me in 1956. "A cartoonist is not the same as an artist. A cartoonist knows the shortcuts and tricks—how to do things in a hurry. His work might have been comic, but it wasn't convincing.

"The cartoonist had to learn about art. So I sent the boys to school. Some of

them hated it and wouldn't go along; most of those fell by the wayside as the studio progressed. But the top men at the studio today are largely those who went through the Disney school."

When a distribution contract with United Artists brought financial stability, the Disney Art School was established at the studio. Don Graham, a teacher at Chouinard, conducted two night classes a week. The opening class in the Disney sound stage on November 15, 1932, attracted twenty-five students. Attendance soon doubled, especially when word spread that Graham was using nude models for the life class.

The fledgling artists did not merely draw static figures, as they had at Chouinard. The models were told to move, and the drawings reflected the progressive poses. Graham knew nothing of animation when he arrived at the studio. He was given a crash course, sitting in the sweatbox for hours as Walt and directors explained aspects of making drawings move. Soon Walt and Graham were critiquing the work of new animators together. Graham began working at the studio full-time, teaching three days and two nights. Field trips were made to the nearby Griffith Park Zoo to sketch animals in movement. Classes were given on color psychology and action analysis. Frank Lloyd Wright, Alexander Woollcott, and other notables came to lecture.

In the six years since the loss of Oswald, the Disney staff had grown from six to 187, including forty animators, forty-five assistant animators, a dozen story and gag men, thirty inkers and painters, and a twenty-four piece orchestra. They were producing nine Mickey Mouse cartoons a year and eight Silly Symphonies. With all the training and instruction that had been going on, it was clear that Walt intended something bigger than the making of short cartoons. That was confirmed one day in 1934 when Walt said to Don Graham: "I need three hundred artists. Get them."

OPPOSITE: *Horace Horsecollar and Goofy in a failed adagio with Clarabelle Cow in* Orphan's Benefit. *Animation drawings.*

LEFT AND ABOVE: *Story sketches for* Mickey's Rival.

CHAPTER FIVE

SNOW WHITE AND THE SEVEN DWARFS

HIS FIRST FULL LENGTH FEATURE PRODUCTION

Walt Disney's
Snow White
and the Seven Dwarfs
in the Marvelous
MULTIPLANE TECHNICOLOR

©WDP

Distributed by RKO Radio Pictures, Inc.

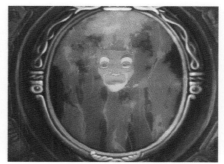

Launching the Animated Feature

One evening in 1934, the chief animators returned to the studio after a dinner at a cafe across Hyperion Avenue. Walt had been awaiting their return, and he seemed to be in a state of unusual excitement. "Come on into the sound stage; I've got something to tell you," he said.

They joined him inside on the bare stage and pulled up folding chairs as Walt stood under the light of a bare bulb. He began telling them the story of Snow White and the Seven Dwarfs. Each scene was acted out, beginning with the dwarfs arriving after a day's work to find Snow White in their cottage. He impersonated each of the dwarfs, hunching down to approximate their size and telling their individual idiosyncrasies. Then he was the wicked queen, eyes flashing as she demanded of the mirror, "Who's the fairest of them all?" The recital continued for two hours until the prince awakened Snow White with a kiss. Even the most hardboiled animators wiped away tears.

"That's going to be our first feature," Walt announced.

The idea for *Snow White and the Seven Dwarfs* had been gestating in Disney's mind for a few years. As a teenager he had been invited along with other Kansas City newspaper delivery boys to attend a performance of the silent movie *Snow White* starring Marguerite Clark. They gathered in the huge Convention Hall, where the movie was projected on screens in the four corners of the auditorium. Walt watched two of the screens, and the performance remained the most vivid memory of his moviegoing childhood.

Walt had long yearned to escape the constrictions of the eight- or nine-minute cartoon, to tell a fully developed story as the other Hollywood studios did. The Snow White fairy tale offered all the elements: romance with an attractive heroine and hero; menace from an evil villainess; comedy and heart with the dwarfs; a happy ending to a timeless folklore story familiar to audiences around the world.

PRECEDING SPREAD: *Picturesque background watercolor of the dwarfs' cottage in* Snow White and the Seven Dwarfs (SPREAD). *Closeup film frame of* Snow White (INSET).

TOP LEFT: *Film frame of Snow White peering in a window of the Dwarfs' cottage.*

ABOVE: *"Magic mirror on the wall. . . ." Film frames.*

ABOVE AND OPPOSITE TOP: *Film frames of* Snow White and the Seven Dwarfs.

Animation drawings of Grumpy (BELOW) *and* Doc (OPPOSITE BOTTOM).

"The figures of the dwarfs intrigued me," Disney recalled in later years. "I thought it was a good plot with wide appeal. It wasn't too fantastic. You can't have too much in a picture that is beyond the realm of your audience's experience."

Disney's decision was economic as well as artistic. Mickey Mouse was an international celebrity as famous as Charlie Chaplin or Greta Garbo, but he wasn't paid as well as his fellow stars. Theater owners allowed only a few dollars for cartoon shorts, no matter how high their quality. Even a huge hit like *Three Little Pigs* brought the studio less than $60,000.

Furthermore, the Disneys had only shorts to sell. Big studios like MGM and Paramount could offer cartoons at a loss as a service to customers of their feature pictures. The Disney studio could not have shown a profit except for the license fee for sales of toys and other products with the Mickey Mouse imprint. Roy Disney was well aware of the dwindling economics of short-subject production, but he was cautious about Walt's plan. So was Walt's wife Lilly. Walt expected *Snow White* to cost $500,000, a huge burden for the small company (the final cost was three times that amount). As usual, he had his way.

Don Graham began the search for the artists Disney needed. Recruiting ads were placed in newspapers up and down the West Coast, then across the nation. Graham spent three months in an office in the RCA Building in New York, poring over portfolios.

Three hundred artists converged on the Hyperion Avenue studio from all over the United States. Unlike the early animators, many had attended four years of college. Some were highly trained as architects and commercial artists who could not find work in Depression America. Disney admitted later that the economic slump proved a boon for the studio; without it, he could never have recruited artists of such high caliber.

The arrivals were sent immediately to school. They were drilled in the drawing of characters, the function of the animation camera, the making of in-betweens (the transitional drawings between those of the animator and his assistant). For two weeks they spent every day drawing in life classes. Then they devoted half a day to drawing, half to the intricacies of production. They were also encouraged to attend night classes, which had grown in attendance to one hundred and fifty. Those who

showed promise after eight weeks of training were assigned to work in the animation department one day a week. The days increased until the newcomers worked full-time.

Walt held regular story meetings to perfect the *Snow White* script. This was something new for the story men: devising an eighty-three-minute movie with brand-new characters instead of inventing gags and business for the studio's stable of cartoon stars. The clarity of Disney's vision is demonstrated in his comments on the scene of the Queen, disguised as the old witch, visiting Snow White at the dwarfs' cottage:

At the time the menace comes in, Snow White should be doing something that shows she is happy and that she is trying to do something nice for these little men. That's the time the menace should strike. It's most powerful when it strikes when people are happy. It's dramatic. . . .

She's taken aback when she first sees the Queen, but [when] there's a lunatic around somewhere and he approaches you, you have a funny feeling. It's nothing you can put your finger on. You wouldn't have the police come, but you'd be on your guard.

That's the point we ought to bring out with the animals. They are dumb, but they have a certain sense like a dog who knows that somebody is not a friend. When the birds see that old witch they know that everything is not right and they're alarmed and back out of the way, retreat quietly. It has just dampened everything.

But when the birds see that the vultures have followed her, that tells them something that even a human won't recognize.

Some of the thought processes that went into animating the dwarfs are illustrated in studio meeting notes:

Dave Hand: There is a hundred feet of the dwarfs walking home from the mine. They are singing the "Hi-Ho" song. We have closeups of the dwarfs in the musical sequence, and we want all their characteristics. George will bring out some of the points about what the dwarfs are doing and the way they are walking. George Stalling: The march home should be a spirit and not a play thing. There is no showoff; the dwarfs do this every day. Doc is leading. He whistles and struts along, waving his hand like a baton. Grumpy takes it as a matter of routine. He turns his head and spits, then goes right back to the song. Happy has a rollicking, rolling movement that is all rhythm. When he comes to a tree stump, he hops over it in a graceful manner. Sneezy is plodding along. Maybe his nose is twitching, maybe he slaps at it. Bashful is walking along in a dreamy attitude, as though he is thinking of something that is unusual to him—a dream, perhaps. Sleepy is almost walking in his sleep, dragging his feet but keeping pace. His pick gets caught in his clothes and forces him to walk on his toes. Dopey tries to keep in step, skips to keep in step, then stumbles and is out of step again.

Seven Dwarfs for Snow White

Disney realized from the beginning that the dwarfs themselves were crucial to the success of *Snow White and the Seven Dwarfs*. Snow White was a charming but standard heroine. The Prince appeared only at the beginning and end of the picture. The Stepmother was a fairy tale villainess. The dwarfs would need to provide most of the comedy and human interest.

The ancient fairy tale offered little help. The dwarfs were phantom figures with no definition. One play version named them Blick, Flick, Glick, Snick, Frick, Whick, and Quee.

Disney assigned the story department to devise seven engaging, easily recognizable characters. The natural thing was to select names that were descriptive. Among the suggestions: Jumpy, Deafy, Wheezy, Baldy, Gabby, Nifty, Swift, Lazy, Puffy, Stuffy, Tubby, Shorty, and Burpy.

Through a process of elimination, the seven finalists were chosen. Those with the obvious characteristics were fairly easy: Grumpy, Happy, Sleepy, Sneezy, and Bashful.

"For the leader, we needed a special kind of personality," Disney commented in 1956. "He was one of those pompous, bumbling, self-appointed leaders who tries to take command and then gets all tangled up. We gave him the name of Doc, since it was a good handle for a person in authority.

"Dopey was the toughest of all. The boys just couldn't seem to get him. They tried to make him too much of an imbecile. Dopey wasn't an imbecile. Finally I thought of a way to put him across: Make him a human with dog mannerisms and intellect.

"That solved it. You know the way a dog will be so intent on sniffing a trail that he doesn't see the rabbit right in front of him—and when the rabbit scurries away the dog does a delayed take? That's the way Dopey was. We made him able to move one ear independently of the other, the way a dog could shake off a fly. And when Dopey had a dream, he pawed with his hand the way a dog does while sleeping.

"But he had to do one thing really well; otherwise he'd just be stupid. So we had him do a clever little slaphappy dance at the dwarfs' entertainment. That let him show off."

The extra effort on Dopey produced results. He proved to be the most beguiling of the dwarfs.

Once the characters of the dwarfs were established, the faces followed with little difficulty. The name dictated the facial expressions to the artists: Happy's face was wreathed in a smile, Grumpy wore a perpetual scowl, Sleepy was droopy-eyed, etc. All had broad cheeks, bulbous noses, white beards (except for Dopey), and wore caps.

The big problem came in animating the dwarfs. Human figures had always proved difficult for animators; now they were drawing ill-formed humans as well. Notes from a meeting of the directing animators illustrate the thought processes in animating the dwarfs:

Dave Hand: "I would like to get an expression of opinion whether we should drive toward the human angle of the dwarfs walking, or whether they should swing from side to side working with their hips."

Bill Tytla: "On account of the pelvis condition, dwarfs are inclined to walk with a swing of the body."

Fred Spencer: "Dwarfs seem to walk with a little waddle. I think we should establish some kind of walk but not make it repulsive."

Fred Moore: "I think we should use a quick little walk, try to work out some pattern where we could get away from the usual way of covering ground."

As the dwarfs began to take physical form, they were fitted with voices befitting their characters. Billy Gilbert, famous for his sneezing routine in vaudeville and movies, was a natural for Sneezy. Roy Atwell, a radio comedian who specialized in mixed-up language, played Doc. Happy was veteran actor Otis Harlan, and Bashful was Scotty Mattraw. The versatile Disney hand, Pinto Colvig, played both Grumpy and Sleepy.

"We tried many voices for Dopey," Disney remarked later, "and every one of them killed the character. So we decided not to let him talk. It wasn't that he *couldn't* talk. He just never tried."

Some of the story men argued that the scene in which Snow White woke up to discover the dwarfs was too long.

"Maybe it is," replied Disney. "But we've got to take the time to have her meet each dwarf individually, so the audience will get acquainted with them. Even if we bore the audience a little, they'll forget it later because they'll be interested in each dwarf."

OPPOSITE LEFT AND ABOVE: Snow White *film frames.*

OPPOSITE RIGHT AND TOP LEFT: *Animation of the homeward march.*

ABOVE: *Animation shows the personality of Snow White.*

TOP RIGHT: *Inking instructions on Dwarf animation.*

OPPOSITE: *Film frames of Snow White's escape through the forest.*

New Tools: Live Action, Multiplane Camera & Effects

From the beginning of animation, the principal figures were anthropomorphic animals and caricatured human beings. Little attempt had been made to present the human form as it really was. The Disney animators faced a problem in making Snow White seem like a real girl.

"It was easy to animate animals," Disney observed. "The audience wasn't familiar with the fine points of how animals move, so we could give a semblance of animal motion and it would be convincing.

"Humans were different. Everyone knows how humans stand and walk and move their heads. If we couldn't duplicate that, we wouldn't have a convincing picture.

"So we tried making movies of live actors doing the things that the animated figures would do. Then the animator could study the film and use it as a guide for his drawing.

"After all, the animator couldn't think up everything in his head. Even such a simple matter as rising from a chair was important. In the old days, a cartoon figure would simply rise to an erect position and walk away.

"But that isn't how people move. By studying live-action film, the animator could see that the figure leaned forward in the chair, placed his hands on the chair arms and pushed himself into a standing position.

"The important thing is to use live action as a guide and not a crutch. When we first started using it, some animators tried to copy the live action exactly. Their work was stilted and cramped.

"The fact is that humans can't move as freely and gracefully and comically as we can make animated figures move. We're not in the business of duplicating live action."

In the 1934 Silly Symphony, *The Goddess of Spring*, an attempt had been made to

portray the goddess Persephone as a realistic girl. The animation was awkward and unconvincing. "We'll get it next time," Disney said confidently.

For *Snow White*, the studio photographed a lithe young dancer, Marjorie Belcher—later known as Marge Champion—whirling and dancing and walking in a costume like the heroine's. Billy Gilbert and other voices of the dwarfs performed before the camera in the flat-footed dance.

The best animators followed Disney's thinking and used live action as a guide. Most of them preferred scenes in which their imaginations could run rampant without concern for lifelike human action. But with the animated feature requiring greater realism, live action became imperative as a reference point.

"No matter how good they are, actors can seldom give you what you want," observed animator Frank Thomas. "You can talk to them and get them thoroughly immersed in the character, but when they do the action, it's not what you have in the back of your mind."

Milt Kahl agreed: "The best use of live action is for ideas—little pieces of movement that an actor does and which do not occur to you. For instance, a couple swirling around on a dance floor. The live action tells you how they move in and out, how the girl's dress twirls, how they move their heads."

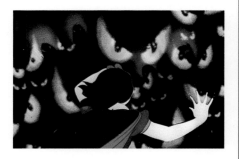

For scenes of rapid or intricate movement, photostats of the movie frames were made so the animator could study them closely. Some kept a moviola by their desks so they could repeat the scene. No matter what device was used, the ultimate interpretation of the scene was through the mind and feeling of the animator as expressed with pencil on paper.

Walt Disney continued using the Silly Symphonies as a proving ground for the advancements he needed for the full-length animated film. To compete with live-action producers, his camera needed to be as fluid as any on a movie set: to dolly in

Disney put the multiplane camera (ABOVE) to the test in a Silly Symphony. He chose a subject called "The Old Mill," which he described as "just a poetic thing, nothing but music. No dialogue or anything. The setting of an old mill at sunset. The cows going home. And then what happens in an old mill at night. The spider coming out and weaving its web. The birds nesting, and then the storm coming up, and the windmill going on a rampage. And with morning the cows come back, the spider web was all shattered, and all that. It was just a poetic thing."
The Old Mill was the most successful Silly Symphony since Three Little Pigs. It won an Academy Award as the best cartoon of 1937 and provided Disney artists an invaluable tool for the first animated feature.

BELOW: Effects animation provides sparkle for the diamonds.

and out of a scene, to photograph foreground actors and background scenery with total realism.

The photography of cartoon backgrounds had changed little since the days of Raoul Barré and Winsor McCay. Drawings of characters were piled like pancakes on scenes of farms or forests or wherever the action took place, and photographed with a stop-action camera. As long as cartoons remained unsophisticated, the system worked satisfactorily. But as Disney sought to match the reality of live-action movies, new methods were needed.

"Our trouble was that we couldn't control the elements at infinity," explained John Hench. He cited the example of a scene with haystacks in the foreground, a farmhouse on a hill with a big moon behind it. As the camera moved past the haystacks and toward the house, the house got bigger, and so did the moon. Said Hench: "We could make the foreground elements bigger, but we couldn't keep the moon the same size."

Another problem. The audience couldn't detect the lack of depth as long as all parts of the picture remained still. But when the foreground trees swept out of camera range as the camera moved in, the trees were exposed as undoubtedly flat.

The solution: the multiplane camera.

As designed by Disney craftsmen, the camera towered fourteen feet and cost $70,000. The camera was stationed above, as with customary animation photography. But instead of layers of art work piled on each other, they were separated onto several glass frames. On the bottom layer could be a row of trees. On the next, a fence. The next might contain the animated layer, perhaps a Prince and Princess walking arm-in-arm. On the top layer, some shrubbery.

The camera could pull in closer and the foreground shrubbery would drop out of the scene. The couple could walk off-screen, and the camera move in further, past the fence and into the trees for a closeup of an owl.

The camera could also be used for a woodland scene with a waterfall. Since the animation of the waterfall required special effects done on a separate frame, the other, static elements of the picture could be placed on separate planes.

Each plane was lighted individually, the lighting adjusted to assure the same colors with each exposure. Bulbs burn blue at their height, red as they wane; so their life span was charted, and the bulbs removed before they reddened.

As part of the preparation for Snow White, Disney established the animation effects department. Scenes of action that are taken for granted in live-action movies—waterfalls, forest fires, lightning, rainfall—are far beyond the skills of even the most gifted of animators. Disney needed to portray such things in order to make features dramatic and convincing.

The Disney researchers went to work. They experimented with colored gels, camera diffusion (blurring focus), filming through frosted or rippled glass, and scores of other techniques. Some of their discoveries were astonishingly simple. Others were too technical to explain to the layman.

Longshot (LEFT) *and closeup* (TOP) *film frames of the housecleaning scene* (ABOVE) *from* Snow White *illustrate how animators used the multiplane camera to achieve depth.*

A *November 1936 story conference concerned the scene of the Witch preparing the poisoned apple:*

Walt: The thought just struck me on the buildup of the music to where she says, "Now turn red, etc." Where it starts you might go into innocent, sweet music while she is saying something about how innocent it looks. The music changes as the apple changes and could stay that way until she says, "Have a bite." It would be a good contrast.

Dave Hand: You mean the innocence of the apple or of Snow White?

Walt: The apple. You have seen the poison seeping into it and the buildup of the hocus-pocus around it. Then some innocent little theme there, coming back to the heavy music after she says, "Have a bite."

Richard Creedon: Admiring the apple as if she'd like to eat it herself—"Pink as a maiden's blush."

The Old Mill, a Silly Symphony, provided the showcase for the discoveries. The animation effects men gave it everything they had: lightning, rain, ripples in water, clouds, sun rays, firefly glow. These things brought fascination to an essentially plotless short subject. Part of the effectiveness of *Snow White* was due to the animation effects: the sparkling jewels in the mine, the horrid concoctions of the witch's brew, the soap bubbles in the washing scene.

"Our business is to present something in an unreal way to make it seem more real," explained Dan McManus, an animated effects veteran. "If you make a pillar of flame the way it really is, it wouldn't look like the real thing. We have to create it as the eye thinks it *should* look."

Lightning, he pointed out, is not convincing if it is drawn exactly as it appears in a photograph. By exaggerating the bolt and filling the screen with intermittent white frames, the effects artist can make his lightning more dramatic than nature's.

Shadows had long posed a problem for animators; the early artists simply ignored them. But shadows were necessary for realism and for dramatic effect.

"Shadows are a lot of trouble," commented effects artist John Reed. "But they are useful. They help create mood. And they lend the illusion that characters have depth instead of being two-dimensional.

"To make shadows, you first of all figure the origin of light. Then you calculate

in what direction and at what angle the shadow will fall. The shadow is done in two ways: by using transparent paint or by painting the shadow black and double-exposing the frame, first with the shadow and then without."

Josh Meador began his Disney career in the effects department with *The Old Mill* and continued through most of the classic films. One of his assignments was to find a way to show mud pots breaking and splashing in the "Rite of Spring" segment of *Fantasia*. He began by stirring an ungodly mess of oatmeal, mud, and coffee grounds in a vat. Air hoses sent bubbles up through it, and the action was captured by high-speed cameras. The individual frames were processed on cels and dyed red against a yellow background. Animation was added to create more splashes and broaden the action. All this was photographed against backgrounds with controlled light intensities. Thus, for a few fleeting seconds on the screen, that audience saw convincing replicas of primeval convulsion of the earth's surface.

Rain had always been drawn in cartoons until the Disney effects department discovered that slow-motion filming of water falling was more convincing. The sprinkles of water were photographed against a dark background and superimposed on the picture. The same with snow. It was really bleached cornflakes photographed against a black backdrop.

Walt: *Something to show how tempting the apple is, how tempting it would be to anyone she offered it to. . . . It would be part of her sales talk here. The apple has just changed from this terrible thing in blowfly colors and the skull to a beautiful red. There wouldn't be too much of it, just enough for contrast.*

OPPOSITE: *Effects add to the horror of the poisoned apple.*

ABOVE: *Using the candle as light source provides dramatic effect.*

ABOVE: *The Disney Studio took special care with its first feature release, even with the press book.*

BELOW: *The dwarfs peering over the cliff as the witch falls to her death.*

"Disney's Folly"

As Snow White pushed into its third year of production, costs continued to mount, and the studio's bankers became increasingly restive. The film trade debated whether audiences would sit still for a feature-length cartoon; it was one thing to amuse them with eight minutes of gags, another to attempt a fully developed plot with serious overtones. There were predictions that "Disney's Folly" would plunge the Disney company, which was forever in hock to the Bank of America, into the bankruptcy court.

Walt Disney continued pressing forward with almost demonic energy. Nothing escaped his scrutiny. He insisted on testing each sequence before it was assigned to animation. Storyboards that portrayed the action in sketches weren't enough. He had story sketches filmed on what became known as a "Leica reel" so they could be viewed in sequence on a movie screen. He also looked at "pencil tests," films of rough animation. He auditioned singers for the leading roles.

Music was important to Disney. Aside from trying to play the violin as a boy, he had no musical education. Yet he had an uncanny ear for what would appeal to the public. He rejected early attempts at songs for *Snow White*. They were Tin Pan Alley tunes designed for diversion from the story, following the formula in Thirties musicals. "We should set a new pattern, a new way to use music," Disney insisted. "Weave it into the story so somebody doesn't just burst into song."

The entire Disney studio worked furiously to complete *Snow White and the Seven Dwarfs* in time for release at Christmas 1937. When Walt viewed the completed film, he noticed a disturbing detail. Something had gone awry in the animation or the camera work so that the Prince shimmied slightly when he leaned over Snow White's glass coffin. Walt told Roy that he wanted to fix the defect; the repairs would cost several thousand dollars. Roy, who had borrowed all he could, decreed, "Let the Prince shimmy." And so the Prince shimmies to this day.

Snow White and the Seven Dwarfs triumphed beyond even the dreams of Walt Disney. Critics praised it to the skies, and it made more money than any film in 1938—$8 million, at a time when the average movie ticket cost twenty-three cents, a dime for children. Defying scoffers who said people would not sit still for eighty-three minutes of drawings that moved, audiences shuddered at the fearful Witch, delighted in the dwarfs, especially Dopey, and cried when Snow White was awakened by the Prince's kiss.

With the release of *Snow White*, Walt at last had the wherewithal, as well as the talent, to thrust the art of animation to greater heights.

TOP: *Film frame of the happy ending.*

BELOW: *Snow White's delight as she watches the dance of the dwarfs.*

CHAPTER SIX
EXPANSION AND WAR

Pinocchio

As the money flowed in from *Snow White and the Seven Dwarfs*, Walt Disney resisted the cry of distributors and theater owners: "Give us more dwarfs!" He used his newfound prosperity to commence with new animated features. *Pinocchio* came first.

It seemed like a natural: an internationally recognized story, a puppet hero who could only be realized in animation, a host of colorful adventures to choose from. With all the pioneering work they had done on *Snow White*, the story men and animators should have had smooth sailing with *Pinocchio*.

For a time it seemed that way. The sprawling tale by Carlo Collodi was trimmed to manageable length, the major characters were designed, the sequences storyboarded, and animation began. Six months later, Disney halted production.

"It isn't working," Disney said. He recognized the lack of endearing characters that had made *Snow White* such an instant success. To remind the audience that Pinocchio was a puppet come to life, he had been animated with simple, almost automated movement, and his face lacked expression. Without a conscience, he performed bad deeds with total innocence. He had none of the boyish humanity that would induce sympathy in his many travails.

Pinocchio was redesigned to make him rounder and more boylike. His nature was altered so that he did bad things only when influenced by evil companions. Because Pinocchio was more or less a blank character, he needed to be surrounded by lively, flamboyant figures. The most important invention was Jiminy Cricket.

Collodi had made the cricket an incidental character who tried to advise Pinocchio to change his ways and then was crushed under the puppet's foot. In the movie, Jiminy Cricket now played a major role as the boy's conscience, trying to steer him back every time he took a wrong turn. Ward Kimball animated Jiminy,

TOP: *The thrilling and dangerous delights of Pleasure Island, in* Pinocchio.

ABOVE: *Walt Disney gave a vivid performance acting out all the characters on a storyboard.*

OPPOSITE: *Effects animation added greatly to the realism of the underwater scenes.*

making him an appealing sage instead of an ugly insect and using carefully selected camera angles so he wouldn't seem tiny. Voiced by Cliff Edwards, who sang the hit songs "When You Wish Upon a Star" and "Give a Little Whistle," Jiminy provided the unifying element for *Pinocchio*.

The Disney artists made ample use of the new toys that had been developed for *Snow White*. The multiplane camera facilitated an opening scene for *Pinocchio* that matched the intricate camera movements of the most skilled live-action directors. The scene sailed over the rooftops of the sleeping village, employing as many as twelve planes. But when the scene ran up a bill of $25,000, Disney blew the whistle and cautioned against such intricate camera work in the future.

Disney was determined that *Pinocchio* would be an even greater achievement than *Snow White*, and he devoted all of his energies to the new production. During a March 1938 story meeting, he expounded on the sequence in which Pinocchio is swallowed by the whale:

"Pinocchio should use every ounce of force he has in his swimming to escape the whale [Monstro]. This should be built to terrific suspense. It should be the equivalent of the storm and the chase of the Queen in *Snow White*. . . .

"The old man [Geppetto, already swallowed by the whale] should get excited

when the whale goes after the fish. When the fish start coming in, he could look toward the whale's mouth and say, 'Tuna!' Pinocchio could be swimming with the fish, and [Monstro] swallows them all. As the old man is fishing inside the whale, he pulls out one fish after another, and finally pulls out Pinocchio without realizing it. The cat [Figaro] sees Pinocchio, gets excited and meows to the old man, but the old man goes on fishing. Finally, Pinocchio calls, 'Father!' The old man recognizes who it is and shouts, 'Pinocchio! My son!'

"We can get comedy out of the whale sneezing with Pinocchio and Geppetto inside. They should react in a certain way—it would be the equivalent to the hiccups in a giant's mouth. . . .

"The underwater stuff is a swell place for the multiplane, diffusing and putting haze in between, with shafts of light coming down. I would like to see a lot of multiplane on this."

The second Disney feature was released in early 1940, and its technical marvels were commended by critics. But it lacked the sentiment and human appeal of *Snow White*, and theater business was disappointing. The start of the war in Europe had wiped out 45 percent of the Disney market, and that contributed to the million-dollar loss on *Pinocchio*, which had cost a staggering $2.6 million.

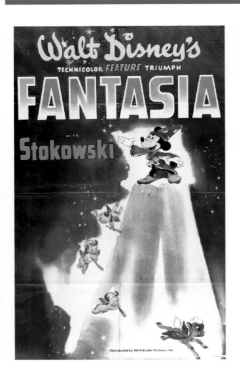

Fantasia

Mickey Mouse had hit a slump, expectable in the careers of movie stars. By the late Thirties his eminence in cartoons had been eclipsed by more surefire Disney comics—Donald Duck, Goofy, and Pluto—as well as other studios' stars such as Popeye and Porky Pig.

Mickey was a throwback to the early years of animation, the time of the Circle Formula and the Rubber-hose Method. He had been rehabilitated in the mid-Thirties by the gifted Freddy Moore. Moore applied the "squash-and-stretch" technique to Mickey, making him more boyish. The body became more pearshaped so it could express emotion; a sunken chest denoted dejection. The head became more flexible; at last Mickey had cheeks. The eyes were placed for better expression. The only thing left unchanged were his ears. Animator Ward Kimball observes: "No matter which way he turns, the ears remain the same. He can make a 360-degree turn and the ears will float in the same position. They're always round, like bowling balls."

Moore changed Mickey's wardrobe as well. No more the two-button shorts and outsized brogans. Now Mickey was dressed in a suit and tie and jaunty hat. The new look made Mickey more accessible but less funny. He had become a supporting player in his own cartoons while his onetime second bananas did the funny stuff.

In 1938 Disney found a new vehicle for his first star. He decided to make a cartoon of *The Sorcerer's Apprentice*, a fairy tale which had been made into a poem by Goethe and a concert piece by Paul Dukas. Disney had been attracted to the music when he heard it at Hollywood Bowl, where he had season tickets. He had started schooling himself in classical music, which he had never found time to listen to before.

Disney bought the rights to the music and cast Mickey as the apprentice whose tampering with his master's powers causes disaster. The short would be done entirely in pantomime; Walt had suspected that his own squeaky voice had contributed to Mickey's decline.

The Sorcerer's Apprentice developed beautifully—in fact, too well. It had cost

TOP RIGHT AND OPPOSITE: *Animation drawings and finished film of* The Sorcerer's Apprentice.

ABOVE: *Baton ready, Leopold Stokowski visits the Hyperion studio to meet with Walt and his staff. With studio musicians Frank Churchill* (LEFT) *and Leigh Harline* (RIGHT).

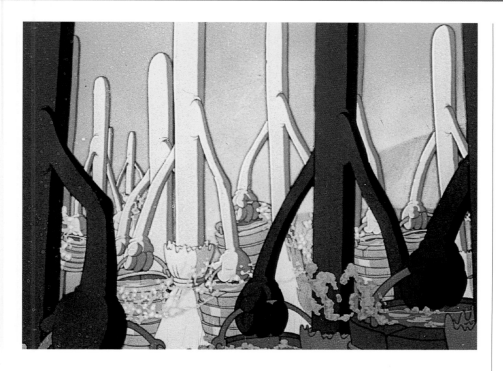

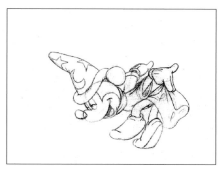

Disney poured more care and expense into The Sorcerer's Apprentice than he had given any short cartoon. Special attention was devoted to the use of color, even the absence of color. The scene in which Mickey misuses the magical powers begins with normal colors. Then the broomsticks begin fetching the pails of water with alarming persistence, and Mickey battles furiously to halt them. He finally hacks them to pieces, and the scene turns to a deathly black and white, which in Technicolor has overtones of dark brown.

Mickey shuts the door behind him with great relief. Then the music begins to thump, like the sound of a revived heartbeat. When the door is opened, a bright yellow shaft of light cuts through the gloom, signifying that life remains in the hacked-up brooms. On they come, marching inexorably forward in the sunshiny glow.

ABOVE: *"Rite of Spring" in* Fantasia *drew praise from critics and scorn from the composer, Igor Stravinsky.*

TOP RIGHT: *Parents complained their children were terrified by the "Night on Bald Mountain" sequence.*

$125,000, which it could never recover if released as a short. What could be done? The answer began when Disney met Leopold Stokowski at a restaurant.

"I understand you are doing *The Sorcerer's Apprentice*," said the famed conductor. "I would love to conduct it for you. I will do it for nothing."

Stokowski came to the studio the next day and became excited when he saw the work that had been done with Mickey and the *Apprentice*. Out of the enthusiasm of Disney and Stokowski came the idea for *Fantasia*, an anthology of serious music illustrated by animation. As the project grew, musicologist Deems Taylor came from New York to act as liaison between the two creators.

As Stokowski explained at the time: "In making *Fantasia*, the music suggested the mood, the coloring, the design, the speed, the character of motion of what is seen on the screen. Disney and all of us who worked with him believe that for every beautiful musical composition, there are beautiful pictures. Music by its nature is in constant motion, and this movement can suggest the mood of the picture it invokes."

Disney and most of the creative staff on *Fantasia* were not students of classical music. They brought to the compositions their own unbridled imaginations, devoid of reverence for the musical score. They first listened to the music and developed storyboards on how the action might take place, allowing their imaginations to soar while keeping the spirit of the compositions. Afterward the music was edited to fit the animation. Such tampering with the classics later brought vituperation from music critics and especially from Igor Stravinsky, the only living composer represented in the score. He never forgave Disney for the editing of "Rite of Spring." As late as 1962 he was complaining about the alterations in the score, adding, "I will say nothing about the visual complement, as I do not wish to criticize an unresisting imbecility."

Some of the selections immediately suggested pictorial themes. Beethoven's *Pastoral Symphony* became a merry romp with fauns, centaurs, centaurettes, and

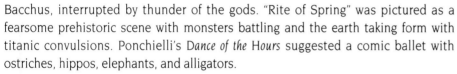

Bacchus, interrupted by thunder of the gods. "Rite of Spring" was pictured as a fearsome prehistoric scene with monsters battling and the earth taking form with titanic convulsions. Ponchielli's *Dance of the Hours* suggested a comic ballet with ostriches, hippos, elephants, and alligators.

Toccata and Fugue in D Minor by Bach was different.

"Here we were dealing with pure music," Disney explained. "There was no story, nothing to go on but our own imaginations. So we would play the music over and over and try to see what images were created in our minds. Perhaps a great crash of music would sound like an ocean wave crashing against the rocks. Then another, and another."

Disney listened to the full symphony orchestra as led by Stokowski in the studio sound stage, then heard it on the playback. The recording was pale and tinny by comparison. He instructed his sound department to develop a multiaural system which could approximate the sound of an orchestra in a concert hall. The result was Fantasound, which recorded the music with several microphones and broadcast it on an equal number of speakers. Thus Disney presaged the era of stereophonic sound in recordings and movies by fifteen years.

Except for "The Sorcerer's Apprentice," all of the music was recorded at the Philadelphia Academy of Music, which had the ideal acoustics. The cost of the music alone amounted to $400,000, and the entire film ran $2.2 million at a time when the average live-action film cost less than a half-million. Theater chains resisted the expensive installations of sound and projection equipment, and *Fantasia* had a limited release in its original form. Eventually the distributor cut the film from two hours to eighty-one minutes, and it played on the lower half of double bills. Without a foreign market, Disney suffered a huge loss, eliminating any plans for *Fantasia* II. Two decades later, a new generation of filmgoers embraced *Fantasia*, with its flights of pure fancy, as a psychedelic trip. Today *Fantasia* is considered by many to be Disney's greatest achievement in animation.

TOP LEFT: *Beethoven's Sixth* (Pastoral) *Symphony provided inspiration for a vision of Mount Olympus.*

ABOVE: *Story sketches for Bach's Toccata and Fugue in D Minor.*

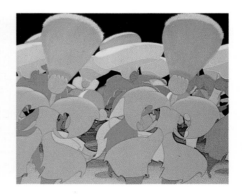

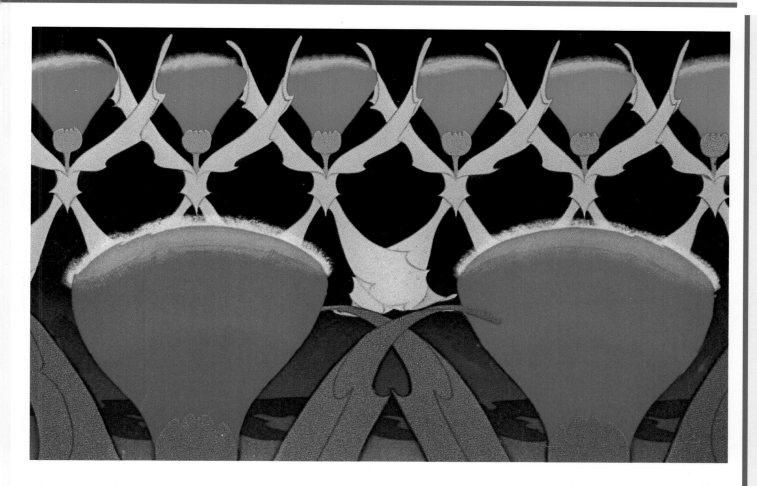

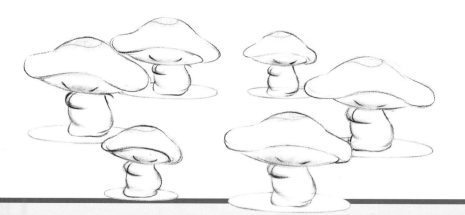

OPPOSITE LEFT: *Leaf and blossom patterns for "The Nutcracker" section.*

OPPOSITE RIGHT AND ABOVE: *The Orchid Girls and Thistle Boys perform a Russian dance in "The Nutcracker Suite."*

LEFT: *Animation of the Mushroom Dancers, depicted as Chinese rice peasants.*

In an early story meeting, Disney outlined his thoughts about the Bambi characters.

"When it comes to the animation, we can do a lot with the rabbit. He has a certain mannerism that can be drawn. We might get him to twitch his nose [he ended up thumping his foot]. . . . I don't like to have us get off the track too much to show his life. Everything should be done through Bambi. . . . The owl ought to be a silly, stupid thing. He is always trying to scare people. I like his crazy screech, as it is described in the book [by Felix Salten]. . . . I would hate to see any of the characters too straight. You would want that in Bambi's mother. You would want Bambi more or less straight in a way. The comedy would come from him as a kid through his questions and his curiosity. The rest of the characters I would like to see come out of life. . . . I would like the Old Stag to say what he has to say in a direct way, and in such a voice that Bambi is unable to answer him. What he says will be sort of final. That can be put over through the voice. . . . I like Faline's character in the book. She is clever and understands things. Bambi asks a lot of questions which she can answer. If we build her up in that way, we will be able to get a lot of stuff over when she and Bambi get together."

ABOVE: Disney studies art work in the early stages of BAMBI.

TOP RIGHT: Model sheet of the mischievous Thumper, who came close to stealing the show.

OPPOSITE: Animators captured the movements of deer by studying the animals at the zoo and the studio.

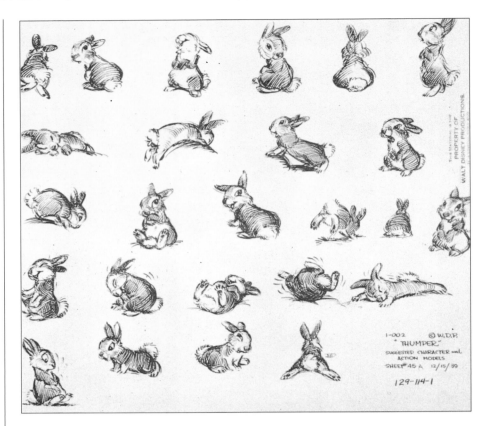

Bambi

The third production in the wake of Snow White, Bambi presented special challenges: the story was far more serious than any the studio had yet undertaken, even tragic, with the death of the deer's mother; the entire cast consisted of animals, and they had to be animated in a natural manner, in keeping with the serious theme of the story. Cartoon characters would destroy the drama.

Disney brought to the studio the painter of animals, Rico LeBrun, who lectured on the structure and movement of animals. Nature photographer Maurice Day spent months in a Maine forest, recording the animals and the changing of seasons. A zoo was established at the studio so animators could study fawns, rabbits, ducks, owls, and even skunks closeup.

Even though no humans appeared in Bambi, live action of human figures was used for reference by animators. Two championship skaters were photographed for the sequence in which Bambi and Thumper skate on a frozen pond.

Despite Disney's hopes to "start moving on the thing and not drag it out too long," Bambi could not be hurried. Unaccustomed to drawing natural animals, expert animators could each manage no more than eight drawings daily, which amounted to half a foot of film, compared to the normal rate of ten feet a day, or less than a second of film vs. over thirteen seconds.

The multiplane camera contributed to the reality of Bambi. The opening shot, as designed by Dick Anthony, was a marvel. The camera roamed through the forest glade, passing trees that seemed amazingly round. The scene of the owl flying through the trees was a masterpiece.

The rain sequence employed color to great advantage. It begins with the young Bambi getting dampened with raindrops as he nestles near his mother. The drops begin to grow in number, and the colors of the forest take on the shadowy gray of rain as the animals scurry to cover. The shower continues and then diminishes. The rain stops, and we see drops fall from a silvery leaf into a forest pool. Reflected in it is a gorgeous rainbow.

Bambi struggled through production and finally reached the screen in August 1942, after America had gone to war. Audiences were seeking more exciting entertainment, and some critics decried Disney's venture into realism. Another crushing loss for the Disney studio.

Economizing: *Dumbo*

One day in the studio parking lot, Disney encountered one of his gifted young animators, Ward Kimball. Walt expounded the plot of a proposed feature, *Dumbo*. Such a recital usually took half an hour or more. This time it was three minutes. That's how simple and straightline *Dumbo* was.

The story of an ugly-duckling baby elephant who redeems himself by learning to fly, *Dumbo* seemed ideal for an inexpensive animated feature. Disney assigned Ben Sharpsteen as supervising director with instructions to avoid the indulgences of *Pinocchio*, *Bambi*, and *Fantasia*.

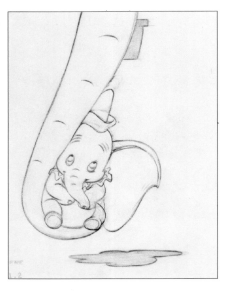

Sharpsteen took his work seriously. Instead of the customary ten feet of work from animators, he insisted on twenty, or more. He prowled the animators' offices, urging them on and banning any frills. He even riffled through their drawings at night, eliminating any in-between work that might slow down production. Ward Kimball had drawn a clever sequence in which a crow nodded in cadence to the music. Sharpsteen discarded the in-between movement, and the crow's head merely turned. Despite the crash schedule—or perhaps because of it—the animators responded with inspired work. *Dumbo* possessed an exuberance that the previous features had lacked. Because it's set in a circus, the film exploded with great flashes of color. But an abundance of reds, yellows, and greens would be too jarring for the eye, so contrasts were made.

One effective scene is staged in silhouette. It pictures the shadows of the circus clowns against the canvas wall as they remove their makeup and costumes. Another sequence shows the elephants and roustabouts struggling in the rain to set up the circus tent. All is gray and murky. Then the sun emerges, and the midway becomes alive with bright colors, the bustling of ticket buyers, the sounds of calliopes and barkers. The sun-drenched colors dramatize the awakening of the circus after the grayness of the rain.

Sharpsteen's economies resulted in a feature that was sixty-four minutes long, ten to twenty minutes short of the customary length. The RKO distributor urged Disney to make it longer, but he refused, explaining that the fragile story could not be stretched. Besides, an additional ten minutes might run a half-million dollars, which the studio couldn't afford. *Dumbo* cost $800,000 and returned an equal amount in profit.

The New Studio, the Strike, and the War

During the expansion of the late Thirties, the Disney Studio on Hyperion Avenue became jammed with more than a thousand workers, triple the number it was first designed for. Production units of *Pinocchio*, *Bambi*, and *Fantasia* as well as the still flourishing shorts were tumbling over each other. Disney was forced to move the *Bambi* unit to a rented building on Seward Street in Hollywood. *Bambi* animators half-seriously called themselves the Foreign Legion, and caricatures of the men in legionnaire uniforms reached Walt. He was not amused.

Roy Disney agreed with his brother that a new studio was necessary. In 1938 they put $10,000 down against the $100,000 purchase of fifty-one acres of flatland on Buena Vista Street in Burbank. Despite the losses on *Pinocchio*, *Bambi*, and *Fantasia*, the Disneys found a willing lender in A. P. Giannini of the Bank of America.

Walt plunged into the planning of the new studio with the thoroughness he applied to feature cartoons. He even examined the design of chairs for the animators. The Animation Building was to be the hub for all operations, connected

OPPOSITE LEFT: *Bill Tytla's animation of the baby Dumbo captures the character's endearing qualities.*

OPPOSITE RIGHT AND ABOVE: *Finished animation.*

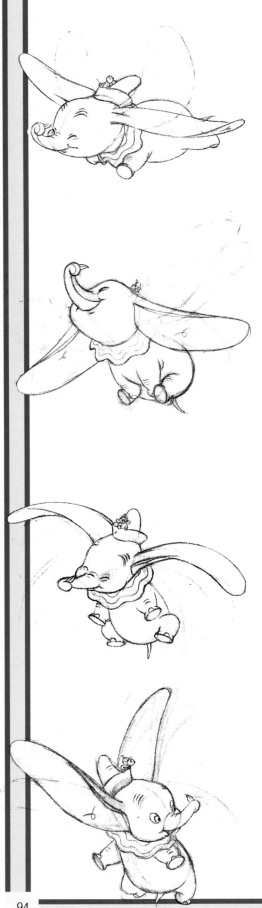

to Ink and Paint, Camera, and Cutting by underground tunnels. The Animation Building would be three stories with eight wings on each floor, connected by a long corridor. The wings were isolated from each other, and some animators complained that such a plan eliminated the collegial atmosphere at the Hyperion studio, where animators mingled easily with each other and with workers in other departments. On the day before Christmas 1939, the exodus from Hyperion to Burbank began. The new studio opened at the worst of times. The war in Europe had started four months earlier.

Strife would soon come to the Disney Studio itself. Walt had planned the Burbank facility to be a workers' paradise, but many of them considered it less than that. Many of the newcomers were dissatisfied with their salaries, the tedium of their work, and the impersonality of the studio.

By the end of the Thirties, all of the talent and crafts at the Hollywood studios had been organized in guilds and unions. At Disney, two unions battled each other and management to organize the workers. One evening, Walt gathered his employees for a remarkable performance in which he traced the sacrifices he and Roy had made to get the studio started, the expansion after *Snow White*, the collapse of the foreign market. He explained how he had rejected easy solutions of abandoning features, cutting salaries, selling control of the company.

He even touched upon his own lack of accessibility: "It's my nature to be democratic. I want to be just a guy working in this plant, which I am. . . . However, I realized that it was very dangerous and unfair to the organization as a whole for me to get too close to everybody."

His pleading failed, and on May 29, 1941, a picket line appeared at the studio. The strike was bitter and acrimonious, shattering the benign image the Disney studio had presented to the world. Frustrated and angry and unwilling to

compromise, Walt accepted the U.S. government's invitation for a goodwill tour of South America in June of that year. He took along animators and story men, and the trip resulted in two lively features, *Saludos Amigos* and *The Three Caballeros*.

When Disney came back from South America, the strike had been settled by government conciliation which made the studio a union shop. Bitterness remained on both sides, and the intimacy and trust Walt had shared with his animators was gone forever.

On the afternoon of December 7, 1941, a few hours after the Japanese had bombed Pearl Harbor, the United States Army moved into the Disney studio. For eight months, it was used as a supply depot for the antiaircraft installations in the mountains surrounding Los Angeles. Walt abandoned plans for features of *Peter Pan*, *Alice in Wonderland*, and *Wind in the Willows* and turned to training films. The first was for the nearby Lockheed Aircraft Corporation, *Four Methods of Flush Riveting*. It was a success, and orders followed from Canada, U.S. Navy Air, the Agriculture Department, U.S. Army, Treasury Department, and others.

Subjects ranged from *Aircraft Carrier Landing Signals* to *Defense Against Invasion*, a health film. Donald Duck was recruited to persuade Americans to pay their taxes. He also gave Hitler the Bronx cheer in *Der Fuehrer's Face*. Disney made one propaganda feature for general release, *Victory Through Air Power*, which promulgated Alexander de Seversky's theories of aerial bombardment.

The war work helped keep the studio doors open at a time when little income was coming from theaters. The training films also interested Disney in a wide range of technical matters not concerned with entertainment and proved that he and his animators could make complex matters understandable to the general public. But they were "lost years," as Roy Disney later remarked. The Disney studio emerged from the war heavily in debt, with little prospect of recovery in the future.

OPPOSITE LEFT: *"I've seen a peanut stand, I've seen a rubber band. . . . When I see an elephant fly. . . ."* Animation drawings by Bill Tytla.

OPPOSITE RIGHT AND TOP: *Dumbo's expressive face could show sorrow and elation.*

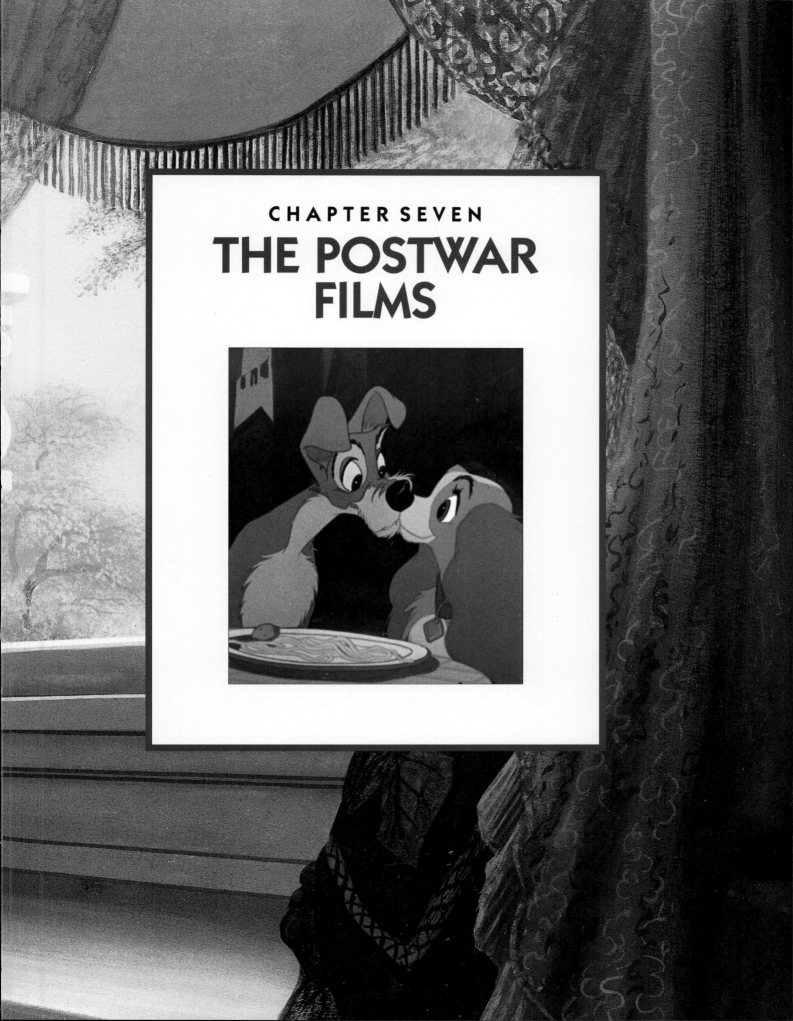

CHAPTER SEVEN
THE POSTWAR FILMS

The Anthology Features

After the war, Roy Disney once remarked, "We were like a bear coming out of hibernation; we were skinny and gaunt, and we had no fat on our bones." The new films reflected that.

The acrid aftertaste of the strike remained, and the company was deeply in debt. Unable to finance a new feature like *Snow White* or *Pinocchio*, Disney launched a series of economical films that brought little glory but much-needed income to the studio.

Make Mine Music was a pop-music vaudeville show with the talents of Dinah Shore, the Andrews Sisters, Nelson Eddy, Jerry Colonna, Benny Goodman, and others. Walt liked the "Peter and the Wolf" episode, but he realized the rest of the film offered no great challenge to his animators.

Disney had long wanted to make a feature based on the Joel Chandler Harris *Uncle Remus* stories he had loved as a child. Because he lacked the money for an animated feature and because of his growing conviction that he needed to move into live-action films, he decided to combine cartoons with a human story about life on a Southern plantation. James Baskett as Uncle Remus told his stories before actual sets painted to look like cartoon backgrounds. After the footage was edited, animators added Br'er Fox, Br'er Bear, and other creatures.

Released in 1946 as *Song of the South*, the film had a modest success. Its importance was largely historical, as a portent of live-action things to come.

In his last major effort to revive his first star's career, Disney reinstated *Mickey and the Beanstalk*, which had been suspended during the war. Donald Duck and Goofy were cast in supporting roles, but again they dominated the comedy. For the first time, Walt Disney was not the voice of Mickey Mouse. Grumbling that his voice was too hoarse, he said to sound effects man Jim MacDonald, "Why don't you do it?"

Mickey and the Beanstalk was combined with a Sinclair Lewis fable *Bongo* for a 1947 release as *Fun and Fancy Free*.

Melody Time in 1948 offered another musical smorgasbord with pop performers; it was noticeable for the raucous "Pecos Bill" episode. The following year brought the last of the anthologies, *The Adventures of Ichabod and Mr. Toad*.

PRECEDING SPREAD: *Detail of the interior of* Lady's *home in* Lady and the Tramp (SPREAD). *Romance blossoms between the mismatched couple* (INSET).

OPPOSITE: *The castle in* Cinderella. *It later inspired the castle at The Walt Disney World Magic Kingdom in Florida.*

TOP LEFT AND ABOVE: *Joel Chandler Harris's* Uncle Remus *stories provided rich comedy for* Song of the South.

Disney on the Fairy Godmother sequence:

"The carriage should be dainty. The wheels shouldn't be enough to hold the weight. We should feel that it's a fairy carriage. . . . Cut out all the excessive dialogue and work on some new dialogue for Cinderella in counter to the melody while she is crying. Have her run out and hit the spot, and as she is saying this, let the animals come up and get closer. Have them gather around in a sympathetic manner. They don't know whether they should approach her or not. . . . Have the miracle happen at the end of the song. "The dream that you wish will come true" is where we start to bring the Fairy Godmother in. She materializes because she is there to grant the wish. The voices come back at Cinderella. Her faith is being thrown back at her. Everybody has gone through a 'the hell with it' feeling."

ABOVE: Cinderella leaves the ball in her "dainty" carriage.

TOP RIGHT: Cinderella's gown.

Cinderella Restores the Glory

The long dry season at the Disney studio ended with *Cinderella*. Work had started on the story before the war, along with *Peter Pan* and *Alice in Wonderland*. Walt had been unable to instill warmth into the characters in *Peter* and *Alice*, but he found *Cinderella* to possess the same qualities as *Snow White*: an engaging heroine in Cinderella, valid villainesses in the guise of the stepmother and the ugly sisters, comic relief with a set of house mice, a well-rounded story with a happy ending.

Disney assigned all of his key story men, directors, and animators to *Cinderella*, and he took part in every story meeting. The directing animation was done by the brilliant Norm Ferguson as well as the "Nine Old Men" (a play on Franklin Roosevelt's epithet for the arch-conservative Supreme Court) who helped create all of the Disney classics from *Snow White* on: Milt Kahl, Frank Thomas, Ollie Johnston, Eric Larson, Les Clark, Marc Davis, John Lounsbery, Woolie Reitherman, and Ward Kimball.

The mice and the cat Lucifer were the inspired creations of Ward Kimball. Walt, who often cast cats as heavies, was dissatisfied with drawing proposals for Lucifer. One day he was visiting Kimball's full-scale railroad train and saw the house cat, a smug, rounded calico. "There's your model for Lucifer," Disney said.

When *Cinderella* was released in June 1950, it was welcomed as Disney's first full-length feature in eight years. With a few dissenters, critics were generally enthusiastic. The postwar generation, many of them with young families of their own, found in *Cinderella* the same kind of euphoric entertainment they had discovered with *Snow White* in their own youths. *Cinderella* had the same comforting message: that good will triumph over evil. And a rollicking song, "Bibbidi Bobbidi Boo," added to the film's popularity. *Cinderella* became Disney's biggest moneymaker, eclipsing even *Snow White*.

Alice, Peter, Lady and the Tramp

Of his unsuccessful *Alice in Wonderland*, Walt Disney told me in 1963: "I think Alice got what she deserved. I never wanted to make it in the first place, but everybody said I should. I tried to introduce a little sentiment into it by getting Alice involved with the White Knight, but they said we couldn't tamper with a classic. So we just kept moving it at circus pace."

No classic ever seemed so ideal for the Disney treatment, and none proved so unworkable. From 1933 on, Disney had tinkered with *Alice*, at times fashioning it for such actresses as Mary Pickford and Ginger Rogers. He bought rights to the John Tenniel illustrations but found they were too intricate to use in animation, except for character design. In story sessions before and after the war, Walt failed to rise to his customary storytelling passion. He simply wasn't enjoying it. Nor did his animators when *Alice* went into production. Productivity sagged, along with their spirits.

"Alice herself gave us nothing to work with," remembers Marc Davis. "You take a nice little girl and put her into a loony bin, and you have nothing. If she had had her cat with her, anything. But she had nothing to work with other than facing

Top: *Alice in Wonderland was technically proficient, but the characters were cold and unappealing.*

Above: *Disney and studio veteran Wilfred Jackson in a story session.*

Disney in a Peter Pan *storyboard conference:*

Don't hesitate to reshoot anything you need. Anything you don't need, don't hesitate to throw it away after you have looked at it. . . . An overlap is never good. Cut close. On the last "See!" you need time for Smee to compose himself before he sticks out his tongue. Then "Woom!" . . . I like the business of Hook getting all dolled up. It's good business. You hear the breaking of the ship and the "Tick Tock." Have a ray of light streaming out of the porthole and the crocodile would be swimming around the water in the stream of light, and at a certain point we would see his eyes. . . . When we get to the fight on the ship, and the croc finally comes in, it would be a nice surprise. . . . I was thinking of the fight—the tempo would pick up and croc's tail would wave faster. Perhaps arrange a few places where Peter might have Hook over the water, and the croc is waiting—but don't slow it up.

one nut after another, one insane person or thing. And that was right through to the end."

"Walt blamed it on us," adds Ollie Johnston. "We blamed it on him. He said, 'You guys didn't get any heart into it; it was too mechanical.' He was right, though it wasn't necessarily our fault. It was everybody's, I guess. Anyway, it has become a cult picture, and now they ask us, 'What were you guys "on" when you worked on *Alice?*' "

Disney was attempting the impossible: to please the Lewis Carroll purists and produce a popular entertainment. British critics assailed the liberties he had taken, and American audiences failed to respond. *Alice in Wonderland* lost a million dollars, wiping out the profit from *Cinderella.*

Peter Pan had been owned by Disney since 1939, and he made several attempts at an animation treatment of the James M. Barrie play. Finally in 1951 he agreed to a story line that closely followed the play, and animation began.

The Nine Old Men and Norm Ferguson (on his last Disney film) realized they could no longer have the benefit of Disney's close participation. He had launched live-action filming in England to make use of frozen funds—money earned in the country that could not be taken out in the tight postwar economy. He was making early preparations for a venture into television. And a new kind of amusement park was forming in his mind. "We knew the moment Walt climbed onto a camera boom, we'd lost him," says Frank Thomas.

Disney still attended storyboard sessions, though his comments were more succinct. Samples: "We don't have the right crocodile yet, it's out of character. . . . Watch so as not to get Hook's teeth too big. . . . Rebuild the Tick Tock scene of Hook. Get expression of fear in his eyes. I don't like the hair-raising. . . . We want to make the music a little more important. I think music will tie it together."

On *Peter Pan,* the animators once again had the use of live action as a guide. As Frank Thomas recalls: "It helped us, and we didn't have to use it if we had a better idea. A lot of stuff we did entirely on our own."

"*Peter Pan* had good imagination and very good characters, and you could get involved in it," adds Ollie Johnston. "Maybe there was less involvement [by Walt] with Peter Pan, but he was the motivation for the picture, so that didn't matter much. Certainly you were involved with Captain Hook and to a lesser extent with Mr. Smee, and a lot with Tinker Bell."

The multiplane camera contributed to some of the best scenes in *Peter Pan.* The first flying sequence over the rooftops of London and around Big Ben required twenty levels of paintings.

The technical innovations and long period of development contributed to the $4-million cost of *Peter Pan.* It was scorned by the Barrie loyalists, particularly for its portrayal of Tinker Bell as a Marilyn Monroe kind of nymphet. But families flocked to the movie, and it restored the Disney reputation, which had been tarnished by *Alice in Wonderland.*

After tangling with two classics, Disney enjoyed working on an original story he could fashion to his own liking. *Lady and the Tramp* dated back to 1937, when it began as a story about a sedate cocker spaniel. In 1943, Disney bought an unpublished short story by Ward Greene about a rowdy, whistling mutt and a lovely, demure cocker spaniel. Not until 1953 did the story take form. It was especially appealing to Walt because it was set in small-town 1910 America and it concerned dogs.

Disney's storytelling skill is illustrated in a meeting about the sequence in which the Tramp kills a rat about to attack the baby at Lady's house.

"Lady's barking, trying to get Jim's [the father] attention, then you see the light coming, his shadow coming up—she's waiting when the door opens. She barks, starts up the stairs, he tries to grab her, says, 'Girl what's the matter?' Jim Dear chains Lady to a dog house out in the rain because of her barking. She has to get Tramp's attention instead.

"She says, 'A rat!' Tramp says, 'Where?' She says, 'Upstairs in the baby's room!' He says, 'How do you get in?' She says, 'The little door in the back.' He runs right through the door in the back. . . .

"It's quick, short things. He'd go right in there. We have this guy cautiously coming up the stairs—remember, he's an *intruder*. He doesn't know which door it is. Then he picks up the scent, and he comes in the room, and there's the baby's crib. We get suspense for a moment. The baby's crib and it's dark. He starts looking around the room, and suddenly he sees two eyes glowing over there. He begins to growl and his hair bristles. You see the form move, and he runs over there.

"It has to be like two guys fighting in the dark and not knowing where the other guy is. A hell of a realistic fight there. We can do it in the shadows from the window onto it—shadow forms against silhouette forms, against the light. Certain lighting effects will make it very effective."

"*Lady and the Tramp* was tough to animate because the dogs were like the deer in *Bambi*: you had to do a realistic, believable animal," says Frank Thomas. "You had

TOP LEFT: *The flying sequence in* Peter Pan *over nighttime* London *was a masterpiece of camera work.*

TOP RIGHT: *The legendary Nine Old Men who animated the Disney classics: (front, left to right),* Woolie Reitherman, Les Clark, Ward Kimball, John Lounsbery; *(rear)* Milt Kahl, Marc Davis, Frank Thomas, Eric Larson, Ollie Johnston.

to have the joints in the right place in the leg, and they had to keep their weight, and you had to keep the right distance from the front leg to the back leg."

Another challenge of *Lady and the Tramp* was using CinemaScope for the first time in an animated feature. Developed by 20th Century-Fox and introduced with *The Robe*, CinemaScope used special lenses to compress filmed images which were then spread out on a wider than normal screen during projection. Layout artists almost had to reinvent their craft. Animators had to remember that they could move their characters across a background instead of the background passing behind them. Scenes could be played with fewer cuts because more characters could be fitted into the broad screen. But the screen had to be filled lest dull patches appear. The result was greater realism but fewer closeups, and hence less involvement with the audience. Despite such drawbacks, the appealing characters and sentimental story of *Lady and the Tramp* found a wide, appreciative audience.

Sleeping Beauty Awakens

Sleeping Beauty ventured boldly into uncharted territory and proved an expensive failure. "I sorta got trapped," Disney admitted afterward. "I had passed the point of no return, and I had to go forward with it."

The film was developing during the mid-Fifties when Disney was enmeshed in Disneyland, the *Mickey Mouse Club*, *Zorro*, and *Disneyland* television shows, and a full program of live-action movies. The *Sleeping Beauty* story men and animators often waited weeks before Disney could meet with them.

The style for *Sleeping Beauty* originated when John Hench observed the famed unicorn tapestries at the Cloisters in New York. Hench bought reproductions

of the tapestries and showed them to Disney. "Yeah," said Walt, "we could use that style for *Sleeping Beauty.*"

Disney assigned Eyvind Earle to paint the backgrounds. Earle had once applied for a job at the old Hyperion studio. Turned down, he spent eleven years in New York building a reputation in the art world. Hired at Disney in 1951, he rose fast as a background painter. For *Sleeping Beauty,* Earle used the best of pre-Renaissance art for inspiration—Dürer, Bruegel, Van Eyck, Botticelli, as well as Persian art and Japanese prints. Earle's landscapes were stylized in primitive technique. "The trees are squared, and everything else carries out the horizontal pattern," he observed at the time. "The hedges, the rocks, the lines of the horizon, all are horizontal. The primitive style never tilts things."

The backgrounds were stunning to the eye but hellish for animators.

"The gothic style was impossible to work with, it was so austere," recalls Frank Thomas. "You couldn't get any life into your characters or your animation. You had to stay within that style."

The animation of the good fairies called for special attention. "I found that when old ladies move, they bounce like mechanical toys," Thomas explained. "They paddle, paddle, paddle on their way. They stand straight, and their arm movements are jerky. Their hands fly out from the body. The reason for all this is that they're afraid to get off-balance, afraid they will fall."

Sleeping Beauty was in production longer (three years) and cost more ($6 million) than any previous Disney feature. The film lacked the humor and personality that Walt could usually endow. It had impressive design and a titanic dragon fight for a climax, but critics called *Sleeping Beauty* pretentious and audiences were unmoved. The film lost money on its first release.

TOP LEFT: *Eyvind Earle's landscapes dominated the style of* Sleeping Beauty.

TOP RIGHT: *Frank Thomas and Ollie Johnston strove to enliven* Sleeping Beauty *with the three good fairies, Flora, Fauna, and Merryweather. Thomas spent time at the supermarket observing rotund old ladies, usually at the dog-food counter, and he also found a model in his children's babysitter.*

ABOVE: *Live action of actors provided a guide for animation of the* Sleeping Beauty *kissing scene, which was less chaste than the one in* Snow White *(page 77).*

ABOVE AND RIGHT: *The spots in* 101 Dalmatians *were an animator's nightmare until Xerox helped provide a solution.*

BELOW: *A press book page from the merchandising campaign for* 101 Dalmatians.

Walt Disney's Last Films

101 *Dalmatians*, released in January 1961, marked the introduction of xerography to the Disney studio. The movie probably couldn't have been made without it. Based on the book by Dodie Smith, it was a landmark in other ways: it was the first Disney animated feature in a contemporary setting; it was the first created by a single story man. Bill Peet was a gifted, headstrong artist and a superb storyteller. He fashioned the 101 *Dalmatians* story on his own, counting on Disney's inattention.

After the Xerox copier appeared on the market, Ub Iwerks, who had developed many technical innovations, adapted Xerox to animation. He fashioned a huge machine that copied drawings onto an electrically charged plate and then onto cels. The technique was perfect for a film in which dozens of spotted dogs appeared on the screen at once. The animators could draw a small group of dogs, and the camera could repeat the group to fill the scene. If the process was done adroitly, the repeats would not be noticed.

Since xerography copied an animator's drawings, for the first time the work could be seen immediately, without the intervention of outlining by an inker. There was one serious drawback: the Xerox machine could not duplicate the animator's delicate lines that endowed unique character; the figures had to be outlined in severe black. Disney believed it was a step backwards to the primitive Twenties before animation had acquired a more sophisticated, elegant look.

But audiences sensed a different, more contemporary appearance in the animation, and 101 *Dalmatians* earned far more than its $4-million cost.

The Jungle Book was the last animated feature in which Walt Disney took part. After the disappointing *The Sword in the Stone*, a fantasy about Merlin and the young Arthur, Disney was determined to give his animators a chance to do their best work. Larry Clemmons was one of the four story men he assigned to the film. Disney

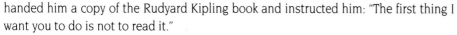

handed him a copy of the Rudyard Kipling book and instructed him: "The first thing I want you to do is not to read it."

The story was built around the Kipling characters, eliminating many of the figures and situations in the 1942 *Jungle Book* movie with Sabu as Mowgli. For years the animators had been drilled in the importance of a clear story line, and Milt Kahl expressed their concern in a meeting with Disney. "You can get all bogged down with these stories," he counseled Kahl. "It will be all right."

Disney was counting on the characters to carry *The Jungle Book*. After hearing Phil Harris perform at a Palm Springs benefit, Walt decided to cast the band leader-singer as the bear Baloo.

"Harris didn't think he could do it, and neither did we," admits Ollie Johnston. "But Walt said he could. After Harris put the lines of dialogue in his own vernacular, why, it just came to life. You know, that deep voice, the friendly attitude the guy has. It was just a pleasure to work with that voice."

Other voices inspired the animators: Sebastian Cabot as Bagheera, the sophisticated panther, Louis Prima as the scat-singing monkey, King Louie, George Sanders as the purringly evil tiger, Shere Khan. As he acted out each role, Walt seemed to be enjoying his sessions with the animators. At the end of one productive meeting he commented: "You guys ought to have me down here more often. I'm the least-paid gag man in the studio."

The Jungle Book was released in October 1967, a year after Walt Disney died. It was a rousing success, with surefire musical numbers such as "The Bare Necessities" compensating for the meandering plot. It was a fitting climax to the Walt Disney era of film animation. During thirty-eight years, Disney and his artists had raised the simple cartoon to the level of rare creativity, producing more than four hundred short cartoons and twenty-three features, of which ten are likely to be seen for generations to come.

TOP LEFT AND ABOVE: **The Jungle Book** *was the last animated film in which Walt Disney participated. The unique voices added greatly to the film's charm.*

BELOW: *"Whoso pulleth out this sword . . . is rightwise King of England."* **The Sword in the Stone.**

CHAPTER EIGHT
THE FILMS WITHOUT WALT

Carrying on the Tradition

The remaining members of the Nine Old Men, along with a few newcomers, continued the string of successes with *The Aristocats* and *Robin Hood*, both competent films though no trailblazers. *The Rescuers*, released in June 1977, was a more impressive achievement, and a proper valedictory. It was the last joint effort by veterans Milt Kahl, Ollie Johnston, and Frank Thomas. As directing animators, they were joined by a newcomer, Don Bluth. Other young recruits, including John Pomeroy, Ron Clements, Glen Keane, and Gary Goldman, were among the character animators.

Walt Disney had acquired the rights to a series of stories by Margery Sharp about an International Rescue Aid Society operated by mice from the basement of the United Nations Building. A screen story had been developed from one of the stories, about the captive of a totalitarian government in a Siberia-like stronghold. Frank Thomas recalls Walt abandoning the project with the comment, "Hell, the politics is pushing our entertainment."

After Disney's death, at least three of the Sharp stories were explored as feature subjects. Finally, a plot was developed about a little orphan girl named Penny who is kidnapped and held in a southern bayou by the villainous Madame Medusa; only someone as small as Penny could enter a cave where a prized diamond had been hidden. Bianca of the Aid Society chooses a shy janitor, Bernard, to help her rescue the girl. Both characters resembled real mice, unlike the cartoony Mickey Mouse. Their characters were enhanced by the voices of Eva Gabor and Bob Newhart.

A pigeon was originally proposed as transportation for the two mice. Then Frank Thomas remembered film taken for the *True Life Adventures* of albatrosses in their hilariously ungainly takeoffs and landings. Captain Orville, brilliantly animated by Ollie Johnston, became the most memorable character of *The Rescuers*. The wryly humorous voice was supplied by Jim Jordan, radio's Fibber McGee.

Madame Medusa was the creation of Milt Kahl. His fellow animators recall that Kahl set such a high standard that his assistants couldn't duplicate his work,

PRECEDING SPREAD: *As with* Robin Hood, Oliver & Company *told a classic story with animal characters. The reworking of* Oliver Twist *made use of contemporary language and music* (SPREAD). *Confrontation of Toon star and private eye in* Who Framed Roger Rabbit (INSET).

OPPOSITE AND BELOW: *After long being relegated to villainous roles in Disney films, cats became the heroes in* The Aristocats.

TOP LEFT: The Rescuers *became a worthy climax to the careers of Disney's Nine Old Men.*

ABOVE: *Between Errol Flynn's and Kevin Costner's versions came Disney's* Robin Hood.

ABOVE AND RIGHT: *The successful* The Fox and the Hound *concerned a fox cub and a puppy who become friends, then find themselves enemies because of the ways of nature.*

BELOW: *Milt Kahl's Madame Medusa followed the Disney tradition of classic villainesses, but her fear of mice diminished her menace.*

and he was forced to draw almost all of Madame Medusa himself. The voice was supplied by Geraldine Page, whom Thomas considers the best of all Disney voices. She had a habit of standing before the microphone, leaning from one foot to the other, then racing around the edge of the studio and returning to the mike to bellow her lines.

Medusa took her place alongside the Witch of *Snow White*, Maleficent, and Cruella De Vil as a classic Disney villainess. Yet Medusa's menace was diffused by one simple scene. When she leaped onto a chair upon seeing the mice, she became a comic villainess, dangerous but less threatening.

The climactic moment in *The Rescuers* comes when Penny, Bianca, and Bernard search frantically for the diamond as the tide rises inside the cave. "But there's hardly any tide in the bayous," someone pointed out in midproduction. After considerable debate, the sequence was animated as written. "Who cares?" said one of the animators. "It's just a cartoon."

The tidal discrepancy went unnoticed by the crowds who patronized *The Rescuers*. Milt Kahl retired after finishing his work with Madame Medusa. Thomas and Johnston developed the characters and animated one sequence for the next feature, *The Fox and the Hound*, then both retired. The new generation took charge.

The Black Cauldron

Four years in production at a record cost for an animated film, *The Black Cauldron* was anticipated as a giant step forward for Disney animation. The adaptation of Lloyd Alexander's *Chronicles of Prydain* promised to offer bold new art by Disney's young generation.

The Black Cauldron came at a time when the Disney management was in turmoil. Film revenues were declining, and the company was seeking to make films for a mature audience, since teenagers scorned anything with the Disney label as

"kid stuff." More threateningly, corporate-raider wolves were circling the faltering company, sniffing for a kill.

In 1979, Don Bluth led a group of young animators out of the studio, declaring that Disney no longer upheld the principles established by its founder. Bluth established his own production company, and his defection had a devastating effect on morale among the young Disney artists. The news signaled trouble within Disney to the public at large, and a flurry of articles speculated on the fall of the House That Walt Built.

Production of *The Black Cauldron* was split into several units, some of which did not communicate with others. There was no strong, guiding hand. Andreas Deja, then a young animator newly arrived from Germany, recalls, "It was a stormy period of change, transition from the old guys to the new guys. There were some guys supervising us who didn't know how to make it happen. Looking back on my drawings for *The Black Cauldron*, I know that I had done many, many better things than those that ended up on the screen." Another new recruit was John Musker, who recalls the general feeling that *The Black Cauldron* would give the new breed "something they could shine on. But once production was rolling, a lot of the younger people believed it was misguided. It was getting too dark, without enough fun aspects. Just too stodgy in many ways. Then it became lethargic in terms of its development, a kind of wavering. A lot of the younger people lost hope in that movie."

Deja had been assigned to conceptual drawings, teaming with Tim Burton, a CalArts graduate with a seemingly inexhaustible imagination. Their efforts never reached the screen. The management gave him complete freedom, Burton remembers.

"I enjoyed that," he says, "but there was the feeling they'd say, 'This is wonderful, but let's not show anybody.'

"I think the company was really at odds with itself. They had this feeling of moving into the future and contemporizing, but they didn't know how to do it. There was a foot in the past and a foot in the future and no firm footing in either. *The Black Cauldron* was one of the things that steered me out of animation."

After attempting a couple of short films, Burton left Disney to become director of *Beetlejuice*, *Batman*, and *Edward Scissorhands*.

TOP LEFT: *The grotesque creatures of* The Black Cauldron *contributed to the film's lack of acceptance.*

TOP RIGHT: *Taran was a credible hero for* The Black Cauldron, *but his adventures proved too labyrinthine for audiences.*

ABOVE: *Spooky conceptual painting by James Coleman.*

TOP: *The new Disney management, headed by Michael Eisner, injected new life into the animation program.*

ABOVE: *Early conceptual art for* The Black Cauldron *by Guy Vasilovich and Ruben Procopio.*

OPPOSITE TOP: *Gurgi was a furry mammal of undetermined species, part hero, part coward.*

OPPOSITE BOTTOM: *The good creature, Gurgi, rescues Taran in* The Black Cauldron.

A New Regime and a Rebirth

As *The Black Cauldron* was nearing completion in 1984, the Walt Disney company underwent a corporate upheaval that resulted in the appointments of Michael Eisner, who had been president of Paramount Pictures, as chairman and Frank Wells, former vice chairman of Warner Bros., as president. The new regime was voted at a meeting of the Disney board on September 24, 1984, and the winning participants met afterward at the Lakeside Golf Club in Burbank for a champagne celebration. Eisner spoke to Roy E. Disney, who had been a prime mover in the change of management.

"Well," said Eisner, "now that this is over, what would you want to do?"

Disney, who had little time during weeks of frantic negotiations to contemplate the future, replied impulsively, "Why don't you give me the Animation Department? Because I'll bet I'm going to be the only guy around here that has any understanding of how it works and what the processes are and who the people are."

Although Roy had never worked in Animation, he had certainly been around it all his life. As the son of the cofounder and nephew of Walt, Roy had spent much of his childhood and his adult life at the Burbank studio. He had made nature films and television movies for the company, and he believed he could help in Animation, drawing on his experience in story and editing. Also he could act as liaison between his friends in Animation and the new, unknown management.

Roy Disney screened the almost finished *The Black Cauldron* and said inwardly, "Oh, God, we've got a problem here." Jeffrey Katzenberg, former production head at Paramount and now chairman of Walt Disney Pictures, had the same reaction. Katzenberg was admittedly unschooled in animation. His entire expertise lay in live-action movies, a totally different discipline. When he suggested that *The Black Cauldron* needed editing to relieve the darkness of the film, the animation people were horrified.

"We can't edit the picture," one of them declared. "It's seamless. It's been made from storyboard to story reel to finished animation, and the seams simply go from one part to another. It's not as if you have coverage that allows you to jump from one place in a movie to another and skip over."

Katzenberg heard their arguments and replied: "Bring the film into an editing room and I will edit it." He removed two or three minutes from the finished film.

Word spread swiftly that the new head of production was actually editing an animated feature. The Philistines had entered the temple! The morale among animators, already at a low ebb, plunged further.

When finally released in July 1985, *The Black Cauldron* was praised by some critics as a brave effort to seek new Disney ground, but others found it dark and forbidding, as did the moviegoing public. Its failure after four years of intense though unguided effort depressed the studio's animators.

Why *The Black Cauldron* failed so spectacularly is still a matter of painful conjecture at Disney.

"It was the most complicated animated movie at its time; it was beautifully done," says Michael Eisner. "But then, I would have spent less time worrying about animating on 70mm and made sure the story worked. . . . It advanced the art of animation, but that art is only as strong as the word. Whether you're in Sophocles' time or the Elizabethan theater or Gilbert and Sullivan or Andrew Lloyd Webber, you've got to have a story and emotion and characters."

Roy Disney agrees: "Story was really the number-one problem. I thought for the first third of the movie it worked pretty well. Then they got to something called the Fair Folk and the main characters got into a cave, and the story just completely stopped going anywhere."

"It was really an admirable attempt at a misguided idea," adds Jeffrey Katzenberg. "The idea, as I learned later, was to make a somewhat darker and therefore more adult movie that would perhaps widen the audience for these films. In fact, it made the fatal error of ignoring its primary audience, which is kids. These [animated] films are not made for kids; they're made for the kid that exists in all of us."

Disney animation artists were further disheartened when management decided to move the entire animation department out of the Animation Building to make room for management and live-action production. Animation assumed quarters in a warehouse two miles away in Glendale.

"So we were moved out of the old studio, and all the traditions were removed at that point," recalls Glen Keane, then a rising young animator. "There was no morgue [storage for past drawings and paintings] to look at, not really unless you drove down to Burbank. There were no more beautiful windows with nice oak trees outside and squirrels running around the college campus.

"We were in a warehouse with wires twisting all around. You got the feeling that 'Boy, we'd better make this thing work. If not, this is it.' It was probably a good thing. It was the equivalent of a kid being let independent by his parents: he doesn't

TOP AND OPPOSITE BOTTOM: *Early conceptual art for* The Black Cauldron *by James Coleman.*

ABOVE: *The sentiment in* Oliver & Company *comes when the Fifth Avenue Jenny adopts the kitten Oliver.*

need their full support anymore." Members of the Animation Department feared the expensive failure of *The Black Cauldron* would prompt the new management to sharply curtail production.

Says John Musker: "I think there was some pressure from certain parts of management just saying, 'These movies cost a lot and they don't return their investment. Here's a movie like *The Care Bears* that didn't cost very much, and it made a lot of money.' I think certain people were saying, 'You really should spend less on these movies and try to get a better profit margin.'" There was also a concern among animation people that Disney's corner on fantasy had been taken over by George Lucas, Steven Spielberg, and other young filmmakers who made startling use of innovative special effects.

"Even *The Black Stallion* could have and should have been a Disney movie," cites John Musker. "There was a feeling at the studio that here were a lot of young people who we thought were really talented, yet there was kind of a lid on them. They admired the films of fifty years ago—*Pinocchio*, *Snow White*, and all those—but there were restrictions keeping that type of film from being made."

Ron Clements suggests another frustration at that time: "There was a stigma about animated films: that they were strictly for kids. We were in our early twenties, and others in our generation were not even aware that Disney was still making animated features. They certainly wouldn't consider going to such films."

Shortly after the new regime had taken over, Roy Disney learned that two bright young directors, John Musker and Ron Clements, had managed to get themselves removed from *The Black Cauldron* and were preparing another feature, *Basil of Baker Street*, a Sherlock Holmes story told with mice. Roy admired what they had done, and he brought Eisner and Katzenberg to see the storyboards.

Katzenberg had seen a storyboard for action scenes in live-action movies, and Eisner had been familiar with storyboards when he was in charge of children's programming at ABC Television. But never had they experienced an entire film told in sketches pinned to boards. They walked from one wing of the building to another to review the boards, which had been left idle for six months awaiting a decision. Eisner and Katzenberg agreed with Roy's enthusiasm for the project. "Let's go with it," they said. And so *Basil of Baker Street*, which became *The Great Mouse Detective*, began production amid vast uncertainty and with a depleted and demoralized staff.

ABOVE: **The Great Mouse Detective** *borrowed its hero and locale from Conan Doyle.*

Roy Disney and Jeffrey Katzenberg began revitalizing the studio's animation, launching a search for new talent that matched Walt's enlistment of artists for *Snow White*. The Animation Department grew from one hundred sixty people to more than six hundred. The company announced that henceforth Disney would release a new animated feature every year, something that Walt had striven for after *Snow White* but could never achieve. No more would the studio put its entire resources into a single film for a three-year period. Two or three projects would be under way at the same time, assuring a yearly release. Budgets would be tight and schedules stringent.

Disney and Katzenberg felt the need for a full-time manager of animation. Katzenberg outlined the qualifications: "Someone who would be able to serve the artists really well, who was going to be very sensitive to talent, who would recognize, as I did from the beginning, that these are not engineers or technicians, they are artists."

After an extensive search, Eisner, Disney, and Katzenberg decided on Peter Schneider, a bright, wiry thirty-five-year-old who had produced plays in London and Chicago and worked for the Arts Festival for the 1984 Los Angeles Olympic Games. Like Katzenberg, he had no background in animation, but he was a quick learner.

The Great Mouse Detective, released in July 1986, proved a happy surprise, filled with humor and inspired animation, and helped immeasurably by the voice of Vincent Price as the archvillain Ratigan. Disney animation appeared to be recovering from the trauma of *The Black Cauldron*.

The recovery was confirmed with the 1988 release, *Oliver & Company*, directed by George Scribner. The story, based on *Oliver Twist* with dogs and a kitten as Fagin's gang, was the first out-and-out comedy among the Disney features. *Oliver & Company* proved that Disney animation could appeal to the teenage crowd. The songs were in the contemporary style, and voicing the characters were such pop stars as Bette Midler, Billy Joel, and Cheech Marin. But despite its success, some Disney animators considered it "another talking dog-and-cat movie."

TOP: *For his scenes with Roger, Bob Hoskins worked with mimes and puppeteers; the animation was added later.*

ABOVE: *Movie magic: Bob Hoskins drives a cartoon car with a cartoon passenger along a real-life boulevard.*

OPPOSITE TOP: *The torchy Jessica Rabbit is described as having "more curves than Mulholland Drive."*

Who Framed Roger Rabbit

The previous Disney regime had bought Gary K. Wolf's whimsical book, *Who Censored Roger Rabbit*, about a movie cartoon character with a real life of his own. Several film treatments were attempted, but the task of combining animation with real-life action seemed impossible. The new management revived the project in 1986 and proposed a coproduction with Steven Spielberg's Amblin Entertainment.

Spielberg sparked to the proposal, but with the proviso that the animation and live action be totally integrated. "If Roger comes into a room and sits down on a big chair," he said, "you should see the cushion go down and a puff of dust. When he sits at a desk, you should see the pencil move and the phone rattle. The action should be completely interactive. The characters should have interactive lighting affected by the environment."

A large order, considering the state of technology. From *Song of the South* on, animation had always been added to live action that had been shot with a stationary camera. But Robert Zemeckis, who had been enlisted by Spielberg and Disney as director, had more ambitious ideas. Peter Schneider recalls: "There were two mandates that Bob Zemeckis brought to the movie: To make this [illusion] work, you must have the cartoon character hold something that is real; second, the camera must move as it does in a live-action movie."

Zemeckis began searching for an animation director who could fulfill his requirements. Then one night in the St. James Club in London, he met Richard Williams, a London-based Canadian who had supplied cartoons for the *Pink Panther* movies and had won an Academy Award in 1972 for *A Christmas Carol*.

"You know," said Zemeckis, "I can't stand the way in *Pete's Dragon* and *Mary Poppins* that those cartoon characters seem pasted on top of the frame."

"I couldn't agree with you more," said Williams. "Forget about the animation. Shoot a modern movie, move the camera, do all the things you'd do if you were shooting *Back to the Future*. We'll make it work."

Their task seemed impossible. The cartoon characters would need to be changed subtly with every camera movement. Zemeckis was certain it could be accomplished with his "one-two punch"—Richard Williams and Industrial Light and Magic. George Lucas's ILM would put the cartoon characters in the frame, darken them and put light patterns over them and perform other optical miracles. A thirty-second test convinced Disney executives, and the project, now called *Who Framed Roger Rabbit*, became a "go" production.

After completion of live-action photography, the Disney animation crew, directed by Dick Williams, took over. There were twenty-five principal animators and a hundred others, enlisted from England, America, Europe, and Australia, in London, creating fifty-six minutes of animation. Another crew in California provided an additional ten minutes.

The vastly complicated production suffered several production slowdowns and cost overruns. In October 1987, Jeffrey Katzenberg summoned the major figures in

the *Roger Rabbit* animation to New York for some tough give and take. The filmmakers returned to their tasks with new resolve, and the fall 1988 release date was met. *Who Framed Roger Rabbit* provided a huge moneymaker and a great leap forward for the animated art. The final sequence, in which the major characters from all the cartoon studios join for a celebration, will remain a landmark of animation.

Triumph: *The Little Mermaid*

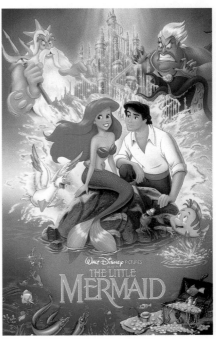

Hans Christian Andersen's "The Little Mermaid" dated back to the late Thirties at the Disney studio. Roy Disney recalls that during the *Fantasia* period Walt mulled a feature that would be composed of vignettes based on the Andersen tales. Kay Nielsen, the art director of the "Night on Bald Mountain" sequence of *Fantasia*, created art work and storyboards for "The Little Mermaid," but the Andersen project was abandoned. Fifty years later, some of Nielsen's art work appeared in the shipwreck scene of Disney's *The Little Mermaid*.

Shortly after the new management took over, twenty members of the Animation Department were summoned to a meeting with Michael Eisner, Jeffrey Katzenberg, and Roy Disney. Each was asked to come with three ideas for an animated feature.

Ron Clements had browsed in a book store and came across a collection of Andersen stories. His suggestion of "The Little Mermaid" sparked immediate enthusiasm. The subject was also welcomed by animators. At last they were free from the constraints of gravity; their characters could swim and dive and twirl in the

TOP: *The Little Mermaid allowed animators to free characters from the restrictions of gravity.*

ABOVE: *Broadway actress Jodi Benson's voice in* The Little Mermaid *helped make Ariel (shown here with Flounder) a spunky heroine.*

water. The underwater ambience seemed inviting, with castles and shipwrecks and a whole civilization under the sea.

John Musker and Ron Clements wrote and directed *The Little Mermaid*, and the producers were Musker and Howard Ashman, who also wrote the lyrics to Alan Menken's songs. Ashman proved a giant contributor to *The Little Mermaid* and later to *Beauty and the Beast*. He was a Broadway craftsman whose most notable success had been *The Little Shop of Horrors*. Jeffrey Katzenberg had admired *Little Shop of Horrors* and had tried to buy the film rights to the Ashman-Menken show. Failing that, he invited Ashman and Menken to work at Disney. Ashman wrote a song for *Oliver & Company*, then he and Menken joined *The Little Mermaid*.

The film required extensive special effects to create the underwater atmosphere. The young animators had worked mostly with animal characters, so much live-action filming was required to key their drawings to human movement. The production schedule was stringent, but deadlines were met. *The Little Mermaid* was a thundering success, selling $84 million worth of tickets in the United States and Canada alone, a record for the first release of an animated feature. Americans bought eight million of the videocassettes.

It was another milestone in rebirth of Disney animation. Musker, Clements, and company had proved that the new breed could create an entertainment that would be embraced by all ages.

The Rescuers Down Under

After the massive outlays of talent, time, and money for *Who Framed Roger Rabbit* and *The Little Mermaid*, Disney theorized that it was time for a simple, inexpensive feature, like the prewar *Dumbo*. A sequel to the 1977 hit, *The Rescuers*, appeared a likely candidate. The company owned the Margery Sharp stories, and no character development would be needed for the two leads, Bernard and Miss Bianca.

Writing began in 1986, with the story set in Australia. *The Rescuers Down Under* proved to be no *Dumbo*. The huge success of recent Disney animated features decreed that future films would need to be major productions. Although Bernard and Miss Bianca had been established, the rest of the characters had to be created.

A new team was formed for *The Rescuers Down Under*. Tom Schumacher, like Peter Schneider, had spent most of his career in theater. He was brought to the studio as producer. Hendel Butoy and Mike Gabriel were given their first directing jobs. Both had come to the studio as animators in the late Seventies.

The Rescuers Down Under benefited from the exotic landscapes and animals, researched by a production team that visited Australia. It also marked the first extensive use of computer technologies which provided unlimited color and more freedom of camera movement. The film was a disappointment at the box office, but it contained stunning visual concepts and superb animation.

As the world entered the last decade of the century, Disney animation had acquired a confidence reminiscent of the *Snow White* era. The situation was similar: young artists with a sense of exploring fresh and exciting vistas, armed with new technologies that made anything seem possible. The Nineties generation was ready for its greatest challenge.

TOP: *Bernard's proposal to Miss Bianca is interrupted by a sudden assignment in Australia.*

ABOVE: *The casting of voices was all-important. Bob Newhart and Eva Gabor agreed to return for the lead roles. But Jim Jordan, hilarious as the voice of the albatross Orville in The Rescuers, had died. A mimic was tested but he lacked the inimitable Fibber McGee quality.*

"Then Roy Disney came up with the idea that Orville would have a brother, Wilbur," says Tom Schumacher. "That solved it, and we thought John Candy would be ideal for the role. He agreed to do it."

CHAPTER NINE
A NEW TRADITION

ABOVE: *The Walt Disney Feature Animation Building at night with the sorcerer's cap illuminated.*

PRECEDING SPREAD: *Belle and the Beast enter the ballroom* (SPREAD). *Finished animation of the enchanted rose* (INSET) *shimmering within the bell jar.*

Renaissance

For many months, travelers on the Ventura Freeway in Burbank puzzled over the peculiar structure rising several hundred yards away. With its strange, hangarlike shape, wide strip of metal across the top, and a large cone out front, it was a mystery. By late 1994, these letters could be seen emblazoned on the side:

A N I M A T I O N

It was the new Walt Disney Feature Animation Building, whimsically designed by Robert A. M. Stern Architects. The cone represented the sorcerer's hat Mickey Mouse had appropriated in *Fantasia*. The metal strip on top—dubbed a "Mohawk" by the building's inhabitants—depicted a strip of film.

The building symbolized the rebirth of Disney animation. It provided comfortable, user-friendly space for the artists who had established a new tradition at Disney. They had produced incredibly successful films that brought recognition by the Academy of Motion Picture Arts and Sciences, critics, and the public that animation could be a major force in both art and entertainment.

"The building is now half the size we need," says Roy Disney, whose office resides in the sorcerer's hat. The animation staff, in fact, has grown to the extent that an old Lockheed Aircraft building is being renovated to accommodate the group. Additionally, a brand new animation facility will open at Walt Disney World in Florida.

The reason for the rebirth? In part it was the awareness of the Disney management that animation was still the heart of the Walt Disney company and needed to be nourished with an infusion of creative and monetary support. There had also been a surge of brilliant young artists from the California Institute of the Arts (CalArts), The School of Visual Arts in New York City, Ringling School of Art and Design in Sarasota, Florida, several other schools, and foreign countries.

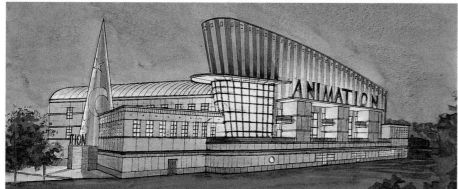

ABOVE: *Roy E. Disney, Vice Chairman of the Board of Disney Enterprises, in his office in the Feature Animation Building.*

ABOVE LEFT: *This 240,000 square foot building serves as the headquarters for the Walt Disney Feature Animation Studio. It recalls the futuristic buildings depicted in early animated movies.*

LEFT: *An architect's perspective of the southwest side of the Feature Animation Building.*

BELOW: *Executive Vice President of Feature Animation Thomas Schumacher.*

"I think it's the public's perception that animation has had a rebirth," observes Thomas Schumacher, executive vice president of Feature Animation. "There was a period of time when for whatever reason—economics or Studio interest—there wasn't much high-quality animation being produced. It wasn't as if we invented something. We simply started working with the same great set of tools again: fabulous music and compelling stories that people can relate to."

But these new animators would have to find their own way. The slump in Disney animation had resulted in a fifteen-year gap in leadership. Most of the Nine Old Men and fellow animators of Walt's classics had died or retired (Eric Larson remained to help train and give sage counsel to new animators).

"I think in some sense, the newcomers were inspired by the filmmakers of the Seventies—the Spielbergs, the Lucases, the Landises, the live-action filmmakers," says Feature Animation President Peter Schneider. "They came along and outdid their predecessors—the Alfred Hitchcocks, the Cecil B. DeMilles. Twenty-year-olds in live-action paved the way. . . . The young animators said, 'We can change things. We know the Disney past, we are steeped in Disney technique and sensibility. Now let's do it our way.'"

Schneider adds that the technique of animation filmmaking is much more advanced than it was ten or fifteen years ago: "The use of the camera and the multiplane, computer imagery, the use of filmic techniques—the audience is very sophisticated about them. They may not be able to tell you about how the camera moves or the use of the color palette, but they respond to it viscerally."

Animation has profited from the new techniques, but Roy Disney cautions: "It will always be about story and character and drama and fun and laughter and tears and music. It will always be about art, and if that ever goes away, that's when it will begin to fail."

Academy Recognition: *Beauty and the Beast*

The tale of *Beauty and the Beast* has been related through the ages. It was a favorite of the French court during the mid-1700s, and the first printed version dates to 1740. For two centuries, writers and artists have offered versions of the ancient fable. Charles Lamb and the Grimm Brothers each interpreted it differently. *Beauty and the Beast* has been portrayed in operas, plays, novels, ballets, a classic Jean Cocteau film, and a television series.

Walt Disney suggested an animated feature of *Beauty and the Beast* as early as 1940, Ollie Johnston recalls. Nothing came of it, perhaps because the romance of a girl and a man-beast seemed too dark and forbidding. With the revival of Disney animation in the late 1980s, *Beauty and the Beast* was reconsidered.

A brand-new team was appointed to guide *Beauty and the Beast*. Don Hahn had been a Disney fan since childhood, haunting Disneyland and watching the movies. After studying music at California State University at Northridge, he joined Disney in 1976 to work on *Pete's Dragon*. He later worked on *Who Framed Roger Rabbit*, first as a cleanup artist and then as associate producer. For *Beauty and the Beast* he was promoted to producer.

Kirk Wise and Gary Trousdale both studied animation at CalArts. At Disney their first codirecting endeavor was a four-minute short for Epcot® in Florida. Both were surprised to be assigned to codirect *Beauty and the Beast*. Several other animators also were promoted from the ranks for important tasks on the film.

Directors Wise and Trousdale were particularly attracted by the unique nature of the title roles. "The Beast himself has almost a dual role of villain and hero,"

Aside from its obvious entertainment values, why did *Beauty and the Beast* capture the admiration of millions of people everywhere? Screenwriter, Linda Woolverton: "Because it's a love story, but more because of the theme: Don't judge a book by its cover; look below the surface."

Producer Don Hahn: "People could relate to the Beast and his longing to find someone to break the spell or accept him for what he was. Or they could relate to Belle and her desire to get out of her little provincial life and into the fairy tales she read about. That, along with the comedy and the music and the sincerity, are what make this picture. Sincerity embodies why these movies succeed, because you really believe these characters on the screen."

Co-Director Gary Trousdale: "My wife tells me it's because *Beauty and the Beast* is every woman's fantasy: To take the guy who is a beast and change him into a prince."

ABOVE: *The Beast and Belle in the garden of the Beast's castle.*

OPPOSITE: *Stained glass windows in the prologue illustrate the Prince's life prior to the curse. Designed by Mac George.*

observes Trousdale. "For the first third or so of the film, he's basically the bad guy. If you know the story, you're supposed to be on his side, but he had a lot to get over."

"When we started out, Belle was essentially the damsel-in-distress model that we've seen in some of the old Disney films," Wise adds. "Maybe a little more worldly-wise than Snow White appeared to be. It was fun to turn a lot of clichés on their ear. The heroine was not necessarily after Prince Charming. The hero was a beast, and the handsome guy (Belle's suitor, Gaston) became the villain."

Since the production of *Snow White and the Seven Dwarfs*, animated features had been crafted directly from storyboard conferences and story sessions, conducted during his lifetime by Walt Disney. Michael Eisner decreed that production of *Beauty and the Beast* would not proceed without a completed script. The task fell to Linda Woolverton. She had written children's plays, young-adult novels, and two unproduced animation-feature scripts.

Woolverton's script provided a structure to build a story on and her initial ideas were visualized, fleshed out, and developed with business and dialogue by directors Wise and Trousdale and a team of story artists led by Roger Allers. Among her many collaborators, Woolverton benefited greatly from work with Executive Producer and Lyricist Howard Ashman.

Ashman proved to be an expert at story construction and character development, reviewing script pages and providing ideas and notes. Woolverton reflects on the work Ashman did with her in New York, "He was a genius. We went

ABOVE: *Early concept art of Belle the heroine.*

BELOW: *Concept art of Lumiere by Supervising Animator Nik Ranieri.*

OPPOSITE ABOVE: *Finished animation of the handsome yet hopelessly vain Gaston.*

OPPOSITE BELOW: *Lumiere, Mrs. Potts, and Cogsworth charm audiences as castle servants attempting to bring Belle and the Beast together.*

IF BEAST STANDS
UP STRAIGHT HE
IS ABOUT 4 HEADS
TALL.

GENERALLY
HE IS HUNCHED
OVER

#4 B

ABOVE: *Analysis of the Beast's structure by Supervising Animator Glen Keane.*

BELOW: *An early sketch of the Beast, by Glen Keane, combining parts of a gorilla and a mandrill.*

through everything—the plot, the characters, everything—daily. We never went out. It was very intense." Among other issues, Ashman solved the vexing problem of the second act, when Belle is held captive in the Beast's castle. He suggested bringing to life the servants who had been rendered into objects by the sorceress's spell. The music and comedy provided by this strategy enlivened the story's otherwise unpromising middle section. Indeed the music by Ashman and composer Alan Menken plays a critical storytelling role throughout this film. "One element that made this movie so successful is that the songs help tell the story," explains Executive Music Producer Chris Montan. "That is the single most important contribution music can make."

Supervising Animator Glen Keane faced the daunting chore of bringing the Beast to life. Son of a newspaper cartoonist and another graduate of CalArts, he animated the bear fight in *The Fox and the Hound*, the villain Ratigan in *The Great Mouse Detective*, and the mermaid Ariel in *The Little Mermaid*. After studying zoo animals and photographs, Keane arrived at this equation for the Beast: face of a mandrill, brow of a gorilla, beard and muzzle of a buffalo, tusks of a boar, neck hair of an ibis, and body of a bear atop the legs and tail of a wolf.

"Beast combines all sorts of wild animals into one character," Keane says, "together with the emotions of a twenty-one-year-old guy who's insecure, wants to be loved, wants to love, but has this ugly exterior and has to overcome this."

Among its many innovations, *Beauty and the Beast* marked a milestone in the use of computer graphics. Head of Story Roger Allers and Story Artist Brenda

Chapman suggested that the crucial ballroom scene, in which Belle and the Beast first signal their love for each other with a joyful dance, could be heightened by computer graphics. Unless "the computer gods frowned" (Trousdale's words), the camera could seem to circle the dancers as in a live-action movie.

"It was a leap of faith for a while," Trousdale remembers. "There had been some use of computer animation before, but nothing on this scale or of such importance. The sequence was kind of a linchpin in the film, a big emotional point; all lines of the film were focused there."

Don Hahn joked grimly that they could end up "with an Ice Capades shot" if the experiment didn't work—the dancers appearing in a moving spotlight against a black background. Fortunately, it worked.

The release of *Beauty and the Beast* in November 1991 created the biggest sensation of any Disney film since *Snow White and the Seven Dwarfs*. Reviews were ecstatic, and *Beauty and the Beast* became the first fully animated film to gross more than $100 million in ticket sales in the United States and Canada (the partly animated *Who Framed Roger Rabbit* grossed $154.1 million).

Beauty and the Beast won a Golden Globe® award for best comedy/musical of 1991. Motion Picture Academy voters included it among the five films nominated for best picture of 1991, marking the first time an animated feature had been so honored. *The Silence of the Lambs* swept the Oscars®, but Alan Menken won for his score, and he and Ashman, who had died March 14, 1991, of complications resulting from AIDS, were honored for their title song.

ABOVE: *The computer-built and rendered three-dimensional ballroom used in the movie.*

BELOW: *An early concept drawing of Cogsworth, the British butler turned mantleclock.*

Magical Splendor: *Aladdin*

From the earliest animation days of the Laugh-O-Grams, Disney has been associated with fairy tales. Surprisingly, only six of the animated features have been based on traditional legends: *Snow White and the Seven Dwarfs*, *Cinderella*, *Sleeping Beauty*, *The Little Mermaid*, *Beauty and the Beast*, and *Aladdin*. To follow the unprecedented success of *Beauty and the Beast* seemed like a daunting task, yet *Aladdin* attracted an even larger audience.

The story of "Aladdin and the Enchanted Lamp" has its origin in a collection of 200 folk tales from the Middle East that became known as *Arabian Nights*. The stories first reached Europe during the early 1700s with a translation from Arabic to French done by Antoine Galland. For two centuries the stories of Aladdin, Sinbad, and Ali Baba fascinated people everywhere.

Disney's *Aladdin* originated in 1988 during the making of *The Little Mermaid*, when Howard Ashman submitted a treatment for *Aladdin* for which he and Alan Menken had written six songs. With *The Little Mermaid* completed, John Musker and Ron Clements began work on a script for *Aladdin*. Ted Elliott and Terry Rossio later contributed to the script.

Production of *Aladdin* began in 1989 with Musker and Clements as directors and producers. One of the first issues to be considered was the depiction of Aladdin himself.

"He went through sort of a metamorphosis," says Musker. "In the early screenings, we played him a little bit younger, and he had a mother in the story.

"We reconceived the character and Aladdin became an orphan living by his wits on the street. And in the design he became more athletic-looking, more filled out, more of a young leading man, more of a teen-hunk version than before. He became seventeen to eighteen rather than thirteen, and the whole romance story was built up more."

Having combined wild beasts for his depiction of the Beast, Glen Keane synthesized Aladdin, using parts of teen idols and movie actors, together with his own memories of romances in high school with girls.

John Musker and Ron Clements recall that Robin Williams' recording of the Genie's dialogue would "go like a house afire, ricocheting off the walls."

"We did five sessions of about four hours each," says Clements, "and he'd pretty much be going the entire four hours. He has a certain kind of energy, like Flubber. When someone else would wear out, he'd suddenly get more energy.

"Usually every session would start out with him a little low-key. Then he'd get wilder and wilder, and by the end he was dripping with sweat and just drained. That wasn't us being taskmasters; that was the way he liked to work."

Mark Henn, who had animated Ariel in *The Little Mermaid* and Belle in *Beauty and the Beast*, brought his third heroine—Jasmine—to life. He works in the animation studio at Disney-MGM Studios in Florida—in full view of theme-park guests—and there he found part of his inspiration for Jasmine. He saw a young park visitor with a long, flowing black mane, and was inspired by her look for his character.

Howard Ashman had envisioned the Genie as a Fats Waller kind of character. Musker and Clements wrote the script with Robin Williams in mind.

Eric Goldberg, who would be animating the Genie, heartily agreed with the Williams casting. He drew a one-minute test, using an old Robin Williams comedy album for a sound track. The test sold the rest of the *Aladdin* team on the concept—and Williams, too.

"Once we knew that Robin was going to do the voice, I felt I had a responsibility to the audience," Goldberg remarks. "The Genie had to deliver, both visually and in terms of humor. We had to go as far as we could go in the animation, so the audience would walk out knowing they had gotten their money's worth."

Animating Williams' comedic gymnastics was no simple task. Goldberg learned that Williams operated two ways: He would read the lines as written, using different voices—Ed Sullivan, Groucho Marx, Peter Lorre, and others—and he would indulge in ad-lib flights of fancy inspired by the story line. Musker, Clements, and Goldberg then chose the nuggets that seemed to work best.

Having animated the realistic figure of Gaston in *Beauty and the Beast*, Andreas Deja was assigned to another villain, Jafar. "This time I'm going to have some fun," he decided. "I don't want to be careful. I'm going to do a design that looks much more grotesque and animatable and interesting and surreal."

The design he created was "almost like a mask that would allow me to be very flexible with the dialogue. His mouth is very low, and he can talk in the corner of his mouth. He had almost monkey-like expressions, which I loved doing."

Deja and his fellow animators faced a problem: How do you compete with the dominating Genie? Deja decided to take the opposite tack and created a dark presence. "I found the more I underplayed his motions and went for subtle animation, the more convincing Jafar became, and the more he contrasted with the other characters."

Richard Vander Wende and Bill Perkins led the team that created the overall look for *Aladdin*. They borrowed from highly stylized Persian miniatures and Arabian calligraphy. They used vivid colors, in the style of *Dumbo* and other early classics.

Aladdin benefited from the services of Disney's Computer Generated Imagery (CGI), which had progressed since the ballroom sequence in *Beauty and the Beast*. CGI allowed Aladdin to take his thrilling carpet ride, the brilliantly textured carpet performing gyrations on a flight through the Tiger Head Cave of Wonders.

Aladdin set a new record for a Disney film: $217.4 million in tickets sales in the United States and Canada alone.

ABOVE: *Jack Skellington in Christmastown.*

BELOW: *Producer Tim Burton poses puppets for giant Polaroids*™.

Innovation: *The Nightmare Before Christmas*

Stop motion—the device by which inanimate objects are made to move on the screen—is almost as old as the motion picture itself. In France, George Melies created many of his trick films by using stop motion. His 1902 A *Trip to the Moon* remains a delight to many.

Filmmakers continued to use stop motion for effects that could not be achieved in live action. *King Kong* is the outstanding example. George Pal's "Puppetoons" amused audiences in the 1940s. With the development of animatronics, stop motion became more sophisticated. Yet not until the computer age could stop motion be employed so successfully to sustain an entire movie.

The Nightmare Before Christmas was the proving ground.

Tim Burton and Henry Selick had become friends when both worked at Disney in the early 1980s. Burton left the Studio to focus on live action, directing *Beetlejuice*, *Batman*, and *Edward Scissorhands*. Selick departed for Northern California to concentrate on stop-motion films.

During his early Disney years, Burton had created a number of bizarre projects, among them a Christmas tale involving a Halloween character named Jack Skellington who tries to take over Christmas. Burton called it *The Nightmare Before Christmas*. Three networks turned it down, and the project was abandoned. In 1990, Burton suggested reviving the idea.

Peter Schneider and Thomas Schumacher took on the responsibility of setting up the infrastructure for Burton to make his movie. "The creative control of the movie

was really left in Tim's hands," says Schumacher. Kathleen Gavin, who had been production manager on *Oliver and Company*, became coproducer on *Nightmare*, providing the link between the Studio and the production team. "It was my role to make sure we got done what needed to be done from a production standpoint," Gavin recalls. "With unique projects that don't fit into our standard production schedule, there are no precedents—you have to figure things out as you go along."

Selick had formed Selick Projects in San Francisco in 1986 and produced numerous features for TV stations, MTV, and commercials. His six-minute film with stop motion and cut-out animation, "Slow Bob in the Lower Dimensions," was widely praised in 1990. Tim Burton admired it and invited Selick to join *The Nightmare Before Christmas* as director.

"We didn't have enough animators, or enough production experience, so we grew into it very slowly," Selick recalls. "We went into production with a couple of animators and a few sets. By the end, we'd grown to twenty stages and about fifteen animators." Shooting stop motion is tedious. The figures have to be moved almost imperceptibly for each shot. The technique requires one image per frame, twenty-four per second, unlike regular animation, which can sometimes get by with "twos"—the same image on two frames. The studio produced one minute of completed film per week.

Although stop motion can create three-dimensional characters and backgrounds that regular animation cannot, there are certain drawbacks. Selick admits, "Whenever you get too close to human acting and design, it really falls flat," he says. "It's especially good when you go into extreme stylization. You could tell a story about humans as long as they're extreme in their designs, like Giacometti's sculptures or Brueghel's paintings. Simple design, almost geometric, as far away from lifelike as can be."

ABOVE: *Concept sketch of musicians in Halloweentown.*

BELOW: *Studies of the Halloweentown trio by Producer Tim Burton.*

ABOVE: *King Mufasa and Simba engage in a playful wrestling match.*

BELOW: *Pumba sketch from a character model sheet.*

Blockbuster: *The Lion King*

Most of Disney's animated features had been based on published material—folk tales, novels, short stories, or plays. *The Lion King* was different. It was entirely original, crafted from storyboards and plotting sessions by Studio artists and writers. Yet if the film struck a reminiscent chord, it was because it touched basic human themes.

"The story has a little bit of Moses, a little bit of Joseph—the prince being exiled from the tribe," observes the Producer, Don Hahn. "Also Hamlet—searching for the murderer of his father and being haunted by his father's ghost.

"It has very much the hero's-journey structure to it, whereby a character is catapulted into growing up by some catastrophic incident in his life. Then he has to go conquer many things, get over many hurdles, seek the wisdom of a wise man and return triumphant to his kingdom."

Such basic human appeal, Hahn believes, helped elevate *The Lion King* to previously undreamed-of heights: domestic gross of $312.8 million; worldwide, $435 million; videocassette sales, 30 million, an industry record. *The Lion King* became the fifth biggest moneymaker in film history.

Two major challenges faced the filmmakers: how to depict the sweeping vistas of the Serengeti Plain and how to animate the animals realistically enough to carry the dramatic story.

Six members of *The Lion King* company, including codirector Roger Allers and Production Designer Chris Sanders, toured East Africa in 1991. They returned with drawings, paintings, and intense feeling for the drama and grandeur of the African wilderness. Story Supervisor Brenda Chapman was among the travelers, and she was

profoundly affected by what she saw. She also picked up the expression "hakuna matata," which provided the title for one of the film's rollicking songs.

Africa became a major character in *The Lion King*. Art Director Andy Gaskill aimed to capture the same majesty of the *Lawrence of Arabia* landscapes, and his color sketches influenced the look of the film.

Not since *Bambi* had Disney animators been faced with the task of creating life-like animals in the wild. The artists visited zoos from San Diego to Miami. Trainers brought a parade of animals to the Studio to be studied and sketched. A biology professor lectured on animal movement. Videos of animal footage and TV nature programs contributed to the wealth of material.

Ruben Aquino, who animated the adult Simba and was the first animator assigned to the film, researched animal locomotion and helped colleagues who came to work on the film later. He explained the difficulty of animating four-legged animals, whose movements in walking and running needed to be lifelike. Animators profited from viewing *Bambi*, *The Jungle Book*, and *Lady and the Tramp*, particularly in the way Tramp tosses remarks as he strolls along.

Having animated Gaston and Jafar, Andreas Deja undertook his third villain with Scar, who ascends to the throne after deposing his brother Mufasa. Deja remembers:

"I listened to the voice tracks of Jeremy Irons, who was playing Scar. My biggest worry was The Jungle Book. I didn't want to compete with the tiger Shere Khan, a similar character, a villain with a British voice (George Sanders); sophisticated, underplayed, above it all. How could you avoid comparisons later on?

"I decided not to look at Shere Khan and purely start from the voice.

"Slowly but surely, Jeremy Irons snuck into the design. All the other animators had a certain way of drawing the lions' manes. Maybe my lion's mane could go backward, as if it were greased."

Deja completed the portrait: "He's skinnier than the other lions, somewhat smoother and slicker in his motions, almost caricaturing, catlike."

ABOVE LEFT: *Scar backs away from an angry Simba during their confrontation at Pride Rock.*

ABOVE RIGHT: *Concept art of Scar by Supervising Animator Andreas Deja.*

LEFT: *Workbook drawing of the Pride Lands by Art Director Andy Gaskill.*

BELOW: *Timon concept drawing by Supervising Animator Mike Surrey.*

ABOVE: *Workbook drawing of Mufasa teaching young Simba how to pounce by Andy Gaskill.*

BELOW: *Rough animation of Nala and Simba by Supervising Animator Ruben Aquino.*

PRECEDING SPREAD: *Color key of the Pride Lands by Background Artist Don Moore.*

"It was a much more realistic and confining setting," observes Hahn. "I remember the directors being frustrated because they had characters with no opposable thumb; they couldn't pick up anything. You've got no props, no costumes, no architecture, no doors to slam, no stairs to walk down. You don't realize how much you rely on those things for business, for acting, for staging. You have all these naked animals on the Serengeti. What do you do?"

The answer came from the filmmakers' use of extraordinary voices and rich dialogue and from Gaskill's art direction.

Tim Rice, who had supplied additional lyrics for Alan Menken's *Aladdin* songs after Howard Ashman's death, joined *The Lion King* in the early stages. When discussion of a composer arose, Rice suggested Elton John, "but he's probably too busy."

To Rice's surprise, John immediately responded to the suggestion. He was a longtime fan of Disney animation, especially *The Jungle Book*. That became evident when John viewed a story reel for his love song, "Can You Feel the Love Tonight."

"The love song was sort of problematic, so we had reduced it to a satiric version sung by Timon and Pumbaa," recalls Roger Allers, who codirected the film with Rob Minkoff.

"When the reel was over, Elton was really upset. We learned from him that the whole reason he got into doing the film was because he loved the love songs in all the Disney pictures. He thought, 'Great! I'm going to get to write a love song for a Disney movie!'

"He spoke very coherently about the values of a love song. We said, 'Okay, we'll give it another try.' To his credit, I think it became much better. We kept the

satiric bookends with the comic characters, but we did it as a love song. I think it helped the picture and the two main characters." "Can You Feel the Love Tonight" won the Academy Award as best song of 1994. Hans Zimmer was also honored with an Oscar for his score.

Computer imagery accomplished something that never could have been possible by animators alone: the stampede of a giant herd of wildebeests.

The scene was pivotal: the villain Scar tries to eliminate his royal brother and nephew, Mufasa and Simba, by trapping them in a wildebeest rampage.

"First of all, it was storyboarded in the traditional manner," Roger Allers relates. "While that was going on, the computer graphics group created a three-dimensional model of a wildebeest in the computer, working from Ruben Aquino's simple drawings from different angles.

"After we were happy with the design of the model, we worked at articulating a walk and a run cycle, making it look natural. That was hard. Building the model and making it work spanned at least a year. A long time.

"Then the paths of action were plotted. Once the backgrounds were designed, the computer department would build simple grid stages that the wildebeests would run on. The camera angle would then be chosen. That gave us the opportunity to run these wildebeests over the camera or below the camera or even to zoom in over them like Zazu flying over the herd.

"Because of the use of the computer we were able to show hundreds of wildebeests. In one scene we had a thousand. To do that by hand would have been impossible."

ABOVE: *During the production of the wildebeest stampede, individual animals were "tagged" with fluorescent colors to make them easier to follow. The hand-drawn Simba animation is by Supervising Animator Mark Henn.*

BELOW: CAPS *combines CGI wildebeests with hand-drawn animation, background art and computer-generated turbulence that looks like dust to create the final product.*

ABOVE: *Concept art of the English settlers' ship by Co-Director Mike Gabriel.*

BELOW: *Early concept drawing of Pocahontas with her friend Redfeather the turkey who did not make it into the movie, by Joe Grant.*

Natural Elegance: *Pocahontas*

It all started at one of the periodic conferences at which any member of the animation department can present an idea for a future project. The presentations last two minutes maximum and result in an immediate turn-down or a go-ahead for further development.

Mike Gabriel made his pitch for *Pocahontas* in early 1991. He had done his homework. He had read all the books, and found the first half of the story of *Pocahontas* ideal for dramatization.

Gabriel had agonized over how to present the story. He arrived at one sentence: "A beautiful Indian princess falls in love with an English settler and is torn between her father's wish to destroy the settlers and her own wish to help them." That message and Gabriel's illustration sold his audience.

For a year Gabriel worked on conceptions for the film with Joe Grant, the legendary Disney artist who had cowritten *Dumbo* and supervised the story of

ABOVE: *Concept drawing entitled "Mystical Meadow" by Bruce Zick.*

ABOVE LEFT: *Color key of the Riverbend.*

LEFT: *Pocahontas spies on John Smith.*

BELOW: *Early experimental animation of Flit by Supervising Animator Dave Pruiksma.*

Fantasia. Eric Goldberg, who had made his Disney debut as a supervising animator for *Aladdin*, joined Gabriel as codirector. Jim Pentacost was brought in as producer and the script was crafted by Carl Binder, Susannah Grant, and Philip LaZebnik.

The artists responsible for the look of *Pocahontas* made a field trip to Jamestown and the surrounding Shenandoah Valley, where the historic events had taken place.

"What struck Art Director Michael Giaimo were very strong verticals and horizontals in the region," recalls Goldberg. "He sought to heighten that in the layout in terms of the tall, tall trees and some extensive flatlands as well.

"We wanted to present the world in a way that was kind of enchanted—so special, so delicate, so wonderful that it would be a shame if something happened to it. Which as you know, does happen in the course of the movie, and is happening to this day."

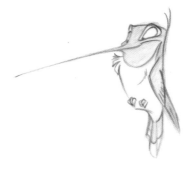

"Animating human beings is probably the toughest thing to do effectively, to give them personality and not make them look like walking mannequins," says John Pomeroy, who returned to Disney in 1992 after a thirteen-year absence.

"The emphasis on acting in Pocahontas seemed greater than in previous pictures," Pomeroy observes, "because so much emphasis was on the love story and making that believable."

The process of achieving the look of John Smith lasted a year. Pomeroy did "miles and miles and miles" of sketches and arrived at an Errol Flynn lookalike. But he looked too clean and well-pressed, so Pomeroy switched to a style more unkempt yet handsome, rugged and skilled in the tricks of the wild. The end result was a combination of the two styles.

"It was necessary not to make him so pumped up all the time," says Pomeroy, "but to give him the physique of someone who had been living in the wilderness or aboard ship."

The animator profited from studying tapes of Mel Gibson's expressions and body movement during recording sessions for the voice of John Smith.

ABOVE: John Smith.

ABOVE CENTER AND RIGHT: Early concept drawing (left) and rough animation (right) of John Smith by Supervising Animator John Pomeroy.

RIGHT: Story sketch by Supervising Animator Glen Keane.

Goldberg and Gabriel admired the way Giaimo used color emotionally rather than photographically. "He can bathe a scene in mauves and pinks if it's a romantic scene," observes Goldberg. "He can go for hot-red and stark color contrasts for a violent scene. He can sap all the color out of it after Kocoum's death."

After his triumph with the Beast, Glen Keane faced a different kind of challenge in animating Pocahontas. The story called for a realistic acting style and subtlety that hadn't been seen in Disney animation. Keane came to the conclusion that most good film actors learn: less is more. The scene in which Pocahontas meets John Smith had been written with dialogue. Keane recalled meeting his future wife in a line at a movie theater and how something magical happened. The Pocahontas scene became simply a meeting of eyes, the background roar of a waterfall the only sound.

"We certainly wanted Pocahontas to be ethnic-looking, to have a definite Native American appearance," says Gabriel. "That gave her a unique look; heroines drawn with the basic cartoon principles of a pretty face tend to look a little bit alike. Glen for a long time pored over Indian faces and really accentuated Pocahontas's Indianness. It took a while to develop sculptured features that still had ethnicity in them."

ABOVE: *Concept art by Art Director Michael Giaimo.*

LEFT AND FAR LEFT: *Final animation of Pocahontas* (FAR) *and Pocahontas with John Smith* (LEFT).

BELOW LEFT: *Concept art of John Smith and Pocahontas among the sunflowers by Michael Giaimo.*

BELOW: *Early character study of Meeko by Supervising Animator Nik Ranieri.*

ABOVE: *Rough animation of John Smith by John Pomeroy. Rough animation of Pocahontas by Randy Haycock.*

ABOVE RIGHT: *Pocahontas at the waterfall where she and John Smith will meet.*

RIGHT: *Meeko and Pocahontas in a scene from "Just Around the Riverbend."*

BELOW: *Rough animation of Governor Ratcliffe by Supervising Animator Duncan Majoribanks. Rough animation of Percy by Animator David Burgess.*

OPPOSITE ABOVE: *Color key of the execution scene by Sunny Apinchapong-Yang.*

OPPOSITE BELOW: *Final animation of the execution scene.*

"A crisp, fresh drawing style influenced the kind of chiseled look we adopted for the characters," says Goldberg. "That also fit with the crisp, clean environment that we were creating. It was one heckuva challenge that we set for our animators and assistant animators. The draftsmanship required of everybody was nothing short of brutal."

Pocahontas constituted a departure for Disney animation. The filmmakers believed that because of the nature of the story and its historic outcome, too much humor would be inappropriate; the ratio of comedy to drama was set at 1:3, a reversal of the usual Disney formula. Almost all of the characters were human, another rare occurrence for Disney. And the traditional happy ending was impossible in view of the historical facts.

No matter. *Pocahontas* became the fourth consecutive Disney animated feature to soar over $100 million in domestic gross.

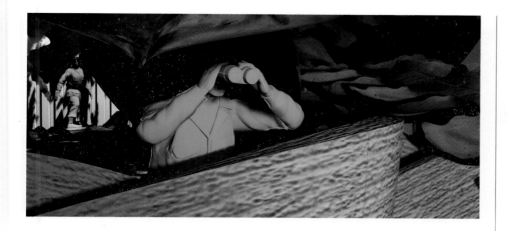

New Dimension: *Toy Story*

"We had a dream of using the computer graphics medium for a feature for over ten years," says John Lasseter.

The dream started in 1984, when Lasseter joined Pixar, the computer graphics studio in San Francisco that had developed techniques for *Star Trek II: The Wrath of Khan, Return of the Jedi,* and other films. A CalArts graduate, Lasseter had worked as an animator at Disney for five years before becoming intrigued with computer graphics. At Pixar, Lasseter followed the example of Walt Disney, who experimented with shorts like "Flowers and Trees" and "The Old Mill" to develop techniques for his first feature. Lasseter and fellow creators honed their computer-imaging skills on such brief films as "Luxo Jr.," "KnickKnack" and the Oscar-winning "Tin Toy."

After the success of "Tin Toy," Lasseter and company decided to launch a feature, *Toy Story,* a tale in which toys would come to life. Walt Disney Feature Animation agreed to sponsor the project. "We were as involved on *Toy Story* as we would be on any of our movies," says Thomas Schumacher. "We were partners with John, we saw every story reel, took part in the casting, the music choices, everything. Because of that, you get the benefit of John's really great original thinking and the benefit of our collective experience in how to get these movies done."

The well-established Hollywood formula of the buddy movie seemed ideal for *Toy Story.* The filmmakers viewed films such as *The Defiant Ones, Midnight Run, 48 Hours,* and *The Odd Couple.* The recipe was the same: two antagonists are forced to combine forces for a common cause.

"I was excited because the buddy picture allowed the characters to grow," says Lasseter. "Our original purpose was for the film, regardless of its story, to have great characters. You come away from a Disney film just loving the characters. Also, we really wanted a comedy. Beyond feeling for the characters, we wanted the audience to laugh with them."

The simple idea of old toy versus new toy gave birth to the tried-and-true Woody, a pull-string talking cowboy (voiced by Tom Hanks), who finds his position as the favorite toy of six-year-old Andy usurped by the hipper Buzz Lightyear (voiced by Tim Allen), a space hero with karate-chop action, laser beams, and pop-out wings.

Like the two leads, the other toys were envisioned as adults. They viewed their purpose of providing pleasure for Andy as a job. Thus the bedroom became a workplace, with all its ramifications: staff meetings, middle management, fear of being laid off.

Many people assume that making an animated feature is faster because of computers. Not so, corrects Lasseter:

"Animation is still filmmaking frame by frame; it still takes a lot of time. Computers don't make it faster. But you can use fewer people. We had 110 people working on Toy Story (versus more than 600 on The Lion King). That was a lean crew: the next film will be bigger, but not by much."

He cautions: "Computers are just tools. Computers don't create anything. The artists do, using computers. There is the assumption that computers create a lot more than they really do. It still takes very talented filmmakers, animators, artists, and technicians with a clear vision to use these tools. The only limit is your imagination."

ABOVE: *Storyboard art by Jeff Pidgeon.*

ABOVE LEFT: *Toy soldiers spy on Andy's birthday party.*

OPPOSITE: *Andy's toys.*

The basic technology was in place, but as the artists came up with new ideas, the technology had to be improved to accommodate them. The Pixar method was to put traditionally trained animators and artists to the task of animating the characters and assign the Ph.D.s in computer science to handle the technical hurdles. As a result, many of the animators were new to this medium. Kathleen Gavin, who came to *Toy Story* fresh from *The Nightmare Before Christmas*, was impressed by the team of newly trained animators. "I think their work in this new medium proves that a good animator is a good animator," says Gavin. "It doesn't really matter if they use a pencil, a computer or a puppet."

John Lasseter explains why he was attracted to the medium he works with:

"Computer animation has one foot in traditional animation and one foot in live-action filmmaking. It is an animation medium, but the tools give you the ability to make things very realistic-looking—dimensional, with the texture of shadows and shading. What you create is a true three-dimensional world.

"As a director, I found I would look at scenes in much more of a live-action way in blocking action, since we're dealing with sets and characters that are like actors and have lots of freedom with the camera. To me the future is that the line between animation and live action will become more blurred.

"This medium is changing by leaps and bounds. In ten years we're going to look back on *Toy Story* and it will seem so simple in comparison to the complex imageries of the future."

Toy Story proved a hit with critics and audiences, the domestic gross climbing to nearly $200 million. On March 25, 1996, the Motion Picture Academy presented John Lasseter with a Special Achievement Oscar for "the development and inspired application of techniques that have made possible the first feature-length computer-animated film."

ABOVE: *Buzz Lightyear concept art by Bud Luckey.*

ABOVE LEFT: *Concept art of Andy's bedroom by Tia Kratter.*

BELOW LEFT: *Concept art of the Dinoco Gas Station by Art Director Ralph Eggleston.*

BELOW: *Woody concept art by Bud Luckey.*

OPPOSITE ABOVE: *Buzz helps Woody during the climactic chase sequence.*

OPPOSITE BELOW: *Aliens welcome Buzz and Woody to their world.*

Classic Adaptation: *The Hunchback of Notre Dame*

Notre Dame de Paris, Victor Hugo's 1831 literary classic, had many attractive elements essential for an animated feature—a powerful story, strong archetypal characters and fascinating settings. The project was espoused by David Stainton, vice president of animation development, who had been a big fan of illustrated classic comic books. The darkly tragic tale of intrigue and betrayal presented a variety of challenges.

Producer Don Hahn and others on the production team discovered that Hugo, who wrote the book at age twenty-eight, had climbed into the bowels of the cathedral and discovered carved in stone the Greek letters of the word "Fate." Says Hahn: "In contemplating those letters and who might have carved them in medieval times, he came up with the character of Quasimodo. Hugo's whole view of the universe in medieval France was much like the medieval view of the universe as a whole, which was: Heaven's above, Hell's below, and man is trapped between. Hugo saw Heaven still above, the streets of Paris as Hell, which they surely were in medieval times, and the person trapped between Heaven and Hell was Quasimodo."

Many members of the *Beauty and the Beast* team joined the film, including directors Kirk Wise and Gary Trousdale. In their search for Disney-style comedic characters, they needed to look no further than Hugo himself.

"One of the things that inspired us about the book was the fact that Quasimodo spoke to the gargoyles as though they were alive," says Wise. "He spoke as though he had a kinship with them, like brothers and sisters. It seemed a natural step for the movie to go the whole nine yards and let the gargoyles be alive, like the objects in *Beauty and the Beast*. The gargoyles' style of humor is a little rowdier, edgier than the style for the objects, because the objects had been human beings. The

ABOVE: *Quasimodo in Notre Dame cathedral. Concept art by Art Director David Goetz.*

BELOW: *Rough animation of Esmeralda by Supervising Animator Tony Fucile.*

OPPOSITE: *The crowd cheers as Quasimodo is crowned the King of Fools.*

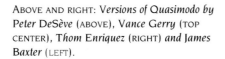

ABOVE AND RIGHT: *Versions of Quasimodo by Peter DeSève* (ABOVE), *Vance Gerry* (TOP CENTER), *Thom Enriquez* (RIGHT) *and James Baxter* (LEFT).

BELOW: *Quasimodo wears the mantle and crown of the King of Fools.*

gargoyles are slightly demonic figures who can be wilder and unpredictable."

Hugo had pictured the heroine Esmeralda as ethereal and exotic. In the movie she becomes fiery, streetwise, a little cynical, but hopeful beneath that.

"She's a Disney girl who has been around the block," Trousdale suggests. "She resorts to underhanded methods if she needs to and doesn't agonize over the moral implications. She's more of a pragmatist."

David Goetz assumed the task of art director for *The Hunchback of Notre Dame.* He and his associates studied all the printed material available, viewed the previous movie versions, and drew inspiration from Hugo's book, which offered an important source of imagery.

Goetz, Wise, Trousdale, and other members of the creative team made a field trip to Paris to research Notre Dame up close. Their most memorable experience was an eight-hour tour by a scholar and author who had written books about Paris history. He contrasted the Middle Ages as it was lived versus the Middle Ages in Hugo's romantic interpretation.

The visitors took photographs and sketched areas of the cathedral where the public was allowed. They were able to find books that documented the restricted areas. A serendipitous find was a book of Victor Hugo's own watercolors.

"It turned out that his paintings were very similar in tone to what we were coming up with for our early visual development work," says Goetz. "It was a kind of moody look that we were playing with. We were a little tentative because it seemed like an un-Disney thing. Then we went to Paris and saw the Hugo paintings and the work of other illustrators of the time. We felt they were so similar that we were really

on a track that was appropriate. Whatever they were thinking at the time was still connecting with us today. We thought, heck, let's go with it."

The cathedral itself is a character with different moods to suit different scenes. Even at its darkest moments, Goetz admits "we've made conscious efforts to keep things light. Also we tried to be theatrical: turning on a spotlight, or artificially lighting scenes. Comedy scenes and musical sequences helped offset the gloom. And there's a lot of fire in the movie."

The Hunchback of Notre Dame presented the ideal situation to work with the animators at Walt Disney Feature Animation (France) S.A. The company had its origin in the Paris-based Brizzi Films, acquired by Disney in 1989.

The twins Gaëtan and Paul Brizzi, born in France to Italian parents, had started drawing at a young age. Seeing *Pinocchio, Dumbo,* and other Disney films fueled their desire to make their drawings move. They started by making five-minute films, later won prizes, and opened their own animation company. Brizzi Films became the biggest animation house in France, making shorts, TV shows, commercials, and one feature. In 1994 the Brizzi brothers were presented with their biggest challenge: producing 10 minutes of final animation for *The Hunchback of Notre Dame.*

Coproducer Roy Conli relocated to France to oversee the production of the French animation team. Together with the Brizzis, Conli led the Studio in storyboarding and producing several sequences of the film including the dramatic opener "The Bells of Notre Dame."

"We don't want to seem pretentious," says Gaëtan Brizzi, "but the directors and the head of layout told us that we brought a French flavor to the film."

ABOVE: *Victor, Laverne, and Hugo sing "A Guy Like You."*

BELOW: *Rough animation of Hugo by Supervising Animator Dave Pruiksma.*

ABOVE: *Storyboard art by Paul and Gaëtan Brizzi of Disney's Paris Studio.*

ABOVE LEFT: *Judge Claude Frollo holds the infant Quasimodo on the steps of the cathedral.*

LEFT: *Quasimodo helps Esmeralda escape.*

BELOW: *Clopin, the self-proclaimed gypsy king, describes the relationship between Quasimodo, Frollo, and the cathedral in the opening prologue's puppet show. This sequence was conceived, animated, and produced by Disney's Paris Studio.*

OPPOSITE: *Background concept of the Cathedral of Notre Dame by Fred Warter, Kathy Altieri, and David Goetz.*

OVERLEAF: *Concept art from Pocahontas.*

How can a feature be made on two continents?

The Brizzis came to Burbank with storyboards and conferred with the animators, layout artists, directors, and others. Back in Paris, the filmmakers remained in contact with America by means of advanced technology. Through satellite and computer systems, they could send their work to Burbank for the scrutiny of character supervisors. They also communicated directly by CLI, Compression Lab Industries' video system by which French artists could present their work to the Studio, a sort of transcontinental conference room.

"Of course it's not as good as being in the same room," says Paul Brizzi. "We'll never replace that, because an artist communicates with his presence, with the way he moves and shows the acting. But it's okay. So far it seems to work."

BOOK TWO

THE MAKING OF HERCULES

CHAPTER TEN

BRINGING HERCULES TO THE SCREEN

ABOVE: *Concept art of Olympus by Rowland Wilson.*

BELOW: *Joe Haidar's original pitch art.*

PART TITLE: *Rough animation of Hercules by Lead Animator Andreas Deja.*

PRECEDING SPREAD: *Concept art of Hercules and Cyclops by Francis Glebas (SPREAD). Final animation of Hercules, Pegasus, and Phil (INSET).*

During the production of Hercules, I visited many of the departments to gain an overview of how a remarkably complex work of animation takes form. To the outsider, it is something of a miracle that the endeavors of so many artists can coalesce, resulting in a single motion picture. The following is the result of my research. —Bob Thomas

Beginnings

In early 1992, thirty artists, writers, and animators waited nervously to present their ideas for new animated features, each show-and-tell limited to two minutes apiece. The first presentation: *The Odyssey*. Their audience deemed it too long, lacking central characters, etc.

Joe Haidar's heart sank. He too was proposing a story from Greek mythology. He felt his chances plummeting. He hoped others would present before him to put some space between *The Odyssey* and his proposal.

Next, Joe Haidar.

An animator with two years' experience at Disney, he nervously announced his subject: *Hercules*. He presented a sketch of *Hercules* and delivered his brief outline. The story is set during the Trojan War, and both sides seek Hercules as their secret weapon. He makes a choice, without considering the consequences. In the end, Hercules learns humility and realizes that might doesn't make right.

Haidar said to himself, "That was a disaster." But at the end of the session, *Hercules*, *The Odyssey*, and one other proposal were chosen for further development. Only *Hercules* survived the development process. Joe Haidar had prepared a page-and-a-half outline, but that was the end of his connection with the project.

Direction: Ron Clements, John Musker

In November 1992, the director-writer team Ron Clements and John Musker were thinking about new ideas for an animated feature. President of Feature Animation Peter Schneider, Executive Vice President Thomas Schumacher, Vice President of Creative Affairs David Stainton and Director of Creative Affairs Jane Healey met with them to review 35 subjects being prepared as possible features. *Hercules* was one of them.

"*Hercules* appealed to us partly because it didn't seem as sacred as something like *The Odyssey*," says Clements. "We had to feel that whatever we chose, we would be able to take quite a few liberties. Hercules was sort of the common man's hero. Another thing that appealed to us was the fact that he was half-god and half-man. The thought that he was caught between the two worlds seemed appealing. Also we were thinking of a kind of superhero—the first superhero."

In early 1994 Musker and Clements began writing treatments. The key elements included a naive hero, worldly-wise heroine, and powerful villain in a battle of idealism versus cynicism. The directors saw Thebes as a Grecian New York City—the Big Olive—beset with troubles and in dire need of a hero.

In preparing the script, Clements and Musker consulted the works of Thomas

Like Walt and Roy Disney, Ub Iwerks and the other Disney pioneers, John Musker and Ron Clements are products of the Midwest. Chicago-born, Musker began cartooning in grammar school, studied animation, and was a cartoonist in high school and at Northwestern University. When his portfolio was rejected by the Disney Studio, he enrolled at CalArts to study the art of animation. In 1977, Musker began working at Disney as an assistant animator on The Small One.

Growing up in Sioux City, Iowa, Ron Clements was beguiled by animation when he first saw Pinocchio at the age of 10. He started making animated films with a Super-8 camera, and later worked part time on commercials for a local television station. Coming to California after high school, he worked for a few months at Hanna-Barbera and studied life drawing at night at Art Center. He was accepted into the Disney animation training program, then apprenticed for two years with Frank Thomas. Rising to animator/storyman, he joined forces with another Disney newcomer, John Musker.

ABOVE: *Directors John Musker and Ron Clements.*

ABOVE LEFT: *Concept art of Hades by John Musker.*

BELOW: *Concept art of Meg by John Musker.*

ABOVE: *This early piece of concept art of Hercules battling Death by Vance Gerry was one of the original ideas for the ending of the film, which was later cut.*

ABOVE RIGHT: *Concept art of the Underworld by Vance Gerry.*

BELOW: *Concept art of Hercules and Phil by John Musker.*

Bullfinch, Edith Hamilton, Robert Graves and other interpreters of Greek mythology. The traditional story of Hercules didn't suit the film's purposes.

First of all, there was the matter of Hercules's birth. The myth declares that the philandering Zeus sired Hercules with an earthling, hence the boy's status as half-man, half-god. Understandably, Zeus's wife Hera became the enemy of Hercules.

"We felt that illegitimacy would be difficult subject matter for a Disney movie," remarks Clements. "So we thought of different ways he could be half-man and half-god. We moved more toward making Hades the villain instead of Hera. The Underworld seemed like such a fascinating, dark image; the contrast of it and Olympus seemed to have all kinds of visual possibilities."

While not keeping to every detail of the original Hercules story, the directors decided to maintain much of the character of the mythical Hercules. "We wanted to keep the impulsive, headstrong, resolute part of Hercules," explains Musker, "and try to fuse it with the innocent hero, the idealist."

They also followed the mythical concept of the hero's journey: immature young man sets off on a quest with the help of a mentor, overcomes impossible obstacles, discovers inside himself the answers he's looking for, and ends up with a maturity he didn't have when he started out.

Hercules's love interest, Megara, evolved into a different kind of Disney heroine: worldly-wise, slightly cynical, like leading ladies in comedies of the 1930s and 1940s.

"We think of her as smarter than Hercules," comments Musker. "She's a step ahead; he has to keep up with her. Some actresses from the Depression era had that quality on the screen; they were tough cookies but could project vulnerability when it was needed. A good combination."

Musker and Clements collaborated on the first draft of the script; at the production phase, more writers joined the creative team. The pair also work together on voice recordings, background, layout, color, and other matters. They divide up sequences and work separately with animators, "though we kibitz back and forth," says Clements.

What happens when they disagree?

"We argue," Clements admits, "and either John will talk me into something or I will talk him into it. We always feel that we're trying to make the same movie. If we do disagree, it's more about how we're going to do something, as opposed to what we're doing."

Producer: Alice Dewey

Alice Dewey, the producer of *Hercules*, was asked if her duties included placating the disparate temperaments of a large assemblage of artists.

"I don't find much temperament at Disney," she replies. "Maybe some. Most people are delighted to be here, care deeply about these movies, and have a passion for the art form. Because of this, there are creative issues that need to be resolved on an ongoing basis. I feel that people here are tremendously genuine about their passion for the work."

Alice Dewey grew up in Wisconsin, attended college there and in Texas, and headed for New York. She worked as stage manager for *Les Misérables*, *Big River*, *Amadeus*, and other shows on Broadway and on the road. Lunch with a friend at Disney led to a job as animation assistant production manager on *The Prince and the Pauper*.

"That was a great way to start: Here I was working on a film with Mickey Mouse," she remarks. "It was sort of like working on an animator's Shakespeare. And I was working with not one but two Mickeys."

Dewey's ascent was rapid: production manager for *Aladdin*, associate producer on *The Lion King*, producer on *Hercules*.

ABOVE: *A reference photo taken during the research trip to Greece.*

BELOW: *Producer Alice Dewey.*

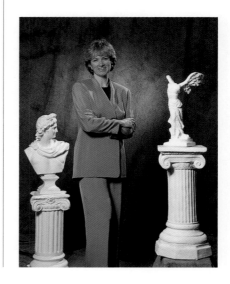

ABOVE: *Concept art of Thebes by Bruce Zick.*

ABOVE AND BOTTOM RIGHT: *Concept art by Hans Bacher.*

What does a producer do?

"A producer in animation tries to guide the movie and all the parts toward the directors' goal. In my mind, we're all here to serve the directors' vision, especially for Ron and John, because they are also writers. They have a really clear idea of what this movie should be. Together with them, we work to staff it, to schedule it and to push and prod it along to make that vision come true."

Early research helps maintain a clear view of where the production is headed. In the initial stages of *Hercules*, Art Director Andy Gaskill illustrated a version of the script. Hans Bacher contributed color styling, and the result proved a valuable vision of what the film might be.

In April 1995, key players journeyed to Greece and Turkey to study the ancient sites they would depict in *Hercules*. For two weeks the producer, directors and department heads soaked in the culture, sights, sounds, smells, and colors. They spent six days in Greece, where they visited Mount Olympus, the Acropolis, Delphi, and Thebes as well as small villages. During their eight days in Turkey, they discovered remarkably well-preserved ancient places. They spent two days on a yacht studying the Turkish coastline and islands. Tombs carved in cliffs provided inspiration for the Underworld.

"It was not only great for the picture to get that kind of reference," Dewey observes, "but also good for us as a team. We came back as a solid group of colleagues ready to make the same movie.

"We saw things together—'Ah, this is the place where we could put Meg's first meeting with Hercules' . . . 'This is what the Underworld might look like.' People were sketching and photographing and shooting video tape. That trip really proved to be a boon to us."

The filmmakers borrowed the fantastic quality of the myths: the larger-than-life personalities, especially the gods; the super-hero quality of the tales; the satyrs, centaurs, harpies, and other wondrous characters well suited to the medium of animation.

"If you look at the literal, written-down story of Hercules, we do depart from it," she adds. "We had a tour guide on the trip who was also a Greek scholar. As we traveled on the bus, he would tell us the stories, particularly about Hercules. He recited the various versions, illustrating that myths are collections of stories. It's an oral history, and those who told it embellished it for their own purposes.

"We thought that was a historian giving us license to tell the story in our own way. We embraced that idea."

ABOVE : *Concept art of Olympus by Francis Glebas.*

BELOW: *Returning home with pictures like this one taken by Layout Supervisor Rasoul Azadani, the artists incorporated elements of the art, architecture, and countryside they saw in Greece.*

ABOVE: *The Muses sing about Hercules. Art from Art Director Andy Gaskill's illustrated script, color by Hans Bacher.*

BELOW: *Composer Alan Menken and Lyricist David Zippel collaborated with the Hercules directors to make the characters sing.*

Music: Alan Menken, David Zippel

"I'm not taking anything else on," Alan Menken had vowed, and it didn't appear that the composer possibly could. He had been preparing a stage version of the hit feature *Beauty and the Beast*, he was finishing the score for *Pocahontas*, composing songs for *The Hunchback of Notre Dame*, as well as preparing a musicalized version of *A Christmas Carol* to be presented in New York.

When Ron Clements and John Musker invited Menken to a meeting about their new project, *Hercules*, he was understandably dubious. The two directors showed him the early art work and outlined the plot. The creative enthusiasm of Clements and Musker was infectious, and Menken began envisioning the score in spite of himself. He felt the desire to compose something almost classically oriented, like *Fantasia*.

Alan Menken teamed up with lyricist David Zippel to create the songs for *Hercules*. Menken and Zippel first collaborated on songs in the late 1970s when both were newcomers to the music business. Zippel had graduated from Harvard Law School and had passed the New York Bar. But having written songs in college, he felt the lure of the theater. He started in cabaret and off-Broadway, then scored a hit with *City of Angels*.

"David has a great Cole Porter-like mind," says Menken. "He loves wordplay, he loves rhymes, there's a sense of freedom and fun. He writes lyrics that encourage the kind of songs that jump out from the story, yet still they forward the plot. They're show-stopping songs."

The songwriters explored territory they had rarely encountered: gospel, rhythm and blues, even a vaudeville song, "One Last Hope," delivered by Danny DeVito in true Jimmy Durante form. "Gospel Truth" evokes the sound of Motown. Two ballads

THALIA

IS HE BOLD??

NO ONE'S BRAVER.

TERPS IS HE SWEET?

MUSES ...OUR FAVORITE FLAVOR!

MMMM... HERCULES...

MEL MY MAN.

(sung by Hercules and Meg) rely on pop style harmonies, yet are specific to the characters that deliver them.

Both songwriters are easterners, with Menken living in northern Westchester, Zippel in New York City. "David comes over and we may have little or no idea when he walks into the room what we'll end up with," Menken says. "He may have a couple of titles in mind, I may have a musical figure in mind. We work and see what feels good. By the time he leaves, there might be a piece of music and maybe a lyric idea.

"David would then go off and write. His lyrics often come back in couplets or small sections—gems of funny ideas. Then he'll pile those together. He may start in the middle and work his way to other analogous places in the song. Somehow, we end up with a song that really works."

When most of the *Hercules* company have finished their work, Menken faces the imposing task of writing the score.

"This score should be an interesting challenge," he remarks. "The songs are very fun, and stylized with gospel, R&B and vaudeville tones. I would like to give the score a real classical quality and also draw on the themes of the songs, translating them into a classical vein.

"In the end I would like *Hercules* to be just the most unique confection. The sense of fun that Ron and John bring to the project has such a power to it. You realize how intrinsic that is to the Disney style."

Lyricist Zippel accompanied the department heads who toured Greece and Turkey in preparation for *Hercules* (Menken was busy completing the *Pocahontas* score and couldn't make the trip). "It gave everyone a sense of what the terrain and the visuals would be," Zippel observes. "Even more important, it became a bonding experience for the creative team. We spent countless hours talking about the project."

He found his greatest inspiration was the diverse and often outrageous characters created by the *Hercules* team.

"I like to work from character—that's the essence of musical theater. Animated features are today's film equivalent of a Broadway show," he comments. "Everything in *Hercules* has a bit of a spin to it. That gave Alan and me the opportunity to write songs that have a cockeyed tilt to them. Nothing is what you'd expect."

ABOVE: *Storyboard art of the Muses' song "Zero to Hero" by Barry Johnson.*

TOP LEFT: *Concept art of Hercules and Phil from "One Last Hope" by Vance Gerry.*

ABOVE: *Gerald Scarfe stands in front of the Feature Animation Building.*

THESE PAGES: *Early in the development process, Gerald Scarfe provided bold and heroic images (*BELOW*) that inspired the style of the film. It wasn't until later that his fluid, powerfully elegant line-work was integrated with the character designs (*TOP RIGHT AND OPPOSITE*).*

RIGHT: *Concept drawings of Zeus.*

BELOW: *Early concept art of Hercules and Pegasus as they stand before Zeus.*

OPPOSITE: *Gerald Scarfe's drawings of various characters: a Theban (*TOP*), Phil (*BOTTOM LEFT*), Hades (*RIGHT*), Pain and Panic (*BOTTOM RIGHT*).*

Production Design: Gerald Scarfe

John Musker vividly remembers a *Time* magazine cover of the Beatles at the height of their fame. As an art student, he admired the bold colors, the sweeping lines and the devilish caricature that captured the look and spirit of the four young revolutionaries. The artist was an Englishman, Gerald Scarfe.

Musker later encountered Scarfe's unique style at a Chicago exhibit of his bizarre sculptures, then in *Pink Floyd—The Wall*, a visualization of the rock group's best-selling album. Scarfe had designed and partially animated the film. Clements also saw Scarfe's work in the designs for the operas *Orpheus in the Underworld* and *The Magic Flute*.

Gerald Scarfe's bold vision and complete irreverence seemed ideal for a film that would take a fresh, comic view of Greek mythology.

"It seemed that his drawing style fit with the whole Grecian-vase painting style we had in mind," comments Clements. "Both have a calligraphic basis with an emphasis on lines."

As Scarfe's conception of the *Hercules* characters began flowing from England to the Studio, the filmmakers were surprised by the size of the drawings. "I didn't realize he drew that big," says John Musker. "It's obvious how much he draws from the shoulder, whereas animation is done close-up, with the wrist. He stands back, which gives real vigor to the drawing."

Scarfe admits to a lifelong fascination with Disney. Asthma kept him confined to bed as a boy, and he passed the time by drawing Disney characters. He was also very intrigued by Greek myths. The first books he bought were a large volume on Greek sculpture and one on Greek mythology. "As far as my own interests and style of art are concerned, it couldn't have been a better subject," he remarks. "In *Hercules*, you're dealing with purely imaginary beings like gods and the creatures of the Underworld instead of human beings in real-life situations."

Scarfe did a minimal amount of research, not wanting to be influenced by other interpretations. He is known in England for his strong, even fierce drawing style, particularly in his political cartoons. "I like to stretch things as far as they will go," he says, "and I like to be as hard as possible on the character."

He began work on sketches, which he sent to Clements and Musker via fax or courier. Not surprisingly, he felt more at ease with figures like Hades, less so with the "cute and cuddly" characters. He pointed out to the directors that in many animated films the main figures receive special care, while the lesser characters and crowd scenes appear less well developed. Scarfe resolved to "pay attention to each character, down to the last person in the crowd."

Hercules amounts to a three-year commitment for Scarfe, who made periodic visits to the Walt Disney Studio for face-to-face meetings. In addition to the hundreds of drawings he created, he reviewed the animators' work for adherence to his concepts.

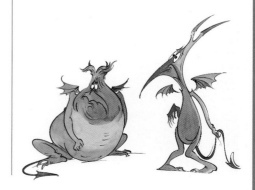

ABOVE: *The Agora.*

THESE PAGES: *Concept art by Andy Gaskill.*

BELOW: *Art Director Andy Gaskill.*

Art Direction: Andy Gaskill

Andy Gaskill enjoyed the good fortune to arrive at the Studio while the first Golden Age of Disney was still flourishing. He had been a sculpture major at the Pennsylvania Academy of Fine Arts in 1973 when he applied for Disney's newly established animation training program. He had the best of teachers: Frank Thomas and Ollie Johnston. Other members of the Nine Old Men still worked at the Studio— "Woolie" Reitherman, Les Clark, Ward Kimball, Milt Kahl, and Eric Larson.

Gaskill began animating on *Winnie the Pooh and Tigger Too* and continued as an animator on other films for five years. Young and restless, he observed the change in the entertainment landscape with innovative films such as *Star Wars*. He felt Disney had become "hopelessly fuddy-duddy" and left to see some of the world.

His work took him to smaller studios, world fairs, theme parks and to Japan to work with Roger Allers on *Little Nemo*. The son of an American soldier and a Japanese mother, Gaskill had spent his first ten years in Japan.

Years later, when Allers was directing *The Lion King* with Rob Minkoff, he called Gaskill and said, "Would you like to do some storyboarding?" Gaskill's second stretch with Disney began.

He planned on a two-week stint, but his work was so well received that he was appointed to the post of art director.

The duties of an art director in animation?

"Technically, you're supposed to be responsible for the over-all look of the

movie: color, style, lighting, and general mood. Whatever the directors want to achieve, you somehow have to interpret and implement.

"But," he adds with a chuckle, "what the art director does is pretty vague."

In the early stages of production, Gaskill does a great deal of drawing, exploring ideas. At some point he relinquishes that work to the people who are actually going to do the drawing—the layout, background, effects, and Computer Graphics Imagery (CGI) people.

"I end up being sort of a nuisance," he jokes, "walking around and asking them to do things." He adds that it's important to have a good relationship which permits him to ask the various artists to try something or to explore a different direction.

From the beginning, the filmmakers sought to integrate Greek drawing and design into the look of *Hercules*. That presented a problem. However beautiful, the restrained and balanced look was too formal to fit into an expressive animation vernacular. Scarfe's work allowed the artists to loosen up and become more outrageous in the design metaphors.

Color styling in *Hercules* aims for the same goal. Many of the sequences are keyed in polar colors—green and orange, blue and red. The result is simple yet vivid.

As art director, Andy Gaskill has found the work he enjoys most.

"One of the things that frustrated me about animation years ago was being in a room all by myself and just drawing," he recalls. "I found that extremely lonely, depressing in an odd way. If I animated a scene that turned out well, it was gratifying.

"Being in a room bugged me. I liked getting out and visiting and schmoozing. I do a lot of that. I'm hardly in my room, ever."

ABOVE: *Nessus, Meg, Hercules, and Phil.*

BELOW: *Meg and Hades.*

Production Styling: Sue Nichols

The organized clutter in the offices of the animation building usually connotes something about the occupant. Sue Nichols' space at the east-facing end of the third floor is marked by rows of tiny fake dime-store trees. "Reminds me of Massachusetts, where my family lives," she explains. "I love the cold." Her window affords a view of the steamy San Fernando Valley.

Both Sue Nichols' parents and a grandfather were artists. When she exhibited a flair for cartooning in school, her father's research revealed the place to learn animation was CalArts. After studying there, she worked at a few production houses in Los Angeles before settling at Disney in 1988, specializing in visual development.

She began in visual development on *Hercules*, moved into story, then returned to graphic styling. Her mission was to assure that the styles of Gerald Scarfe and Bruce Zick (who created early visualizations of backgrounds) were integrated into the Disney style.

Nichols also was concerned that the props, effects and layout worked with the characters. Nichols found herself often conferring with Art Director Andy Gaskill and Head of Layout Rasoul Azadani to be sure the various styles were harmonious.

Nichols created reference guides for all the artists on *Hercules*. They were divided into three parts, a guide to production design, a guide to costuming, and a guide to Greek style.

"Lots of times the research that is done in development gets lost as a production progresses," she observes. "The books comprise all the research we found. For example, you can see the patterns for the costuming: the Doric for peasants, the fancier Ionic for the city folk, and the Corinthian for the gods and the creatures."

Hades

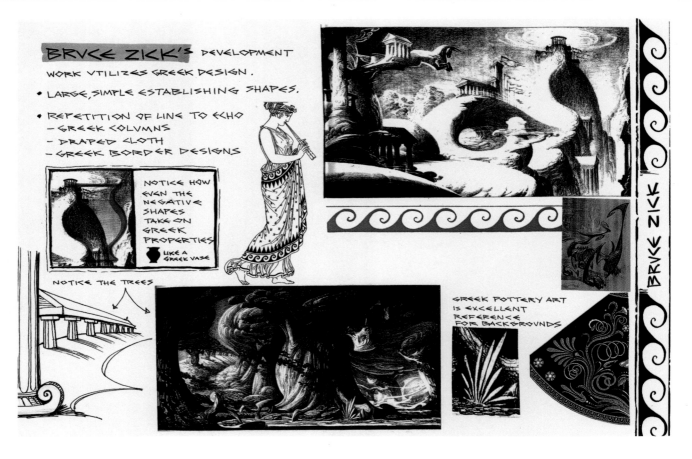

BRVCE ZICK'S DEVELOPMENT WORK VTILIZES GREEK DESIGN.

• LARGE, SIMPLE ESTABLISHING SHAPES.

• REPETITION OF LINE TO ECHO
  – GREEK COLUMNS
  – DRAPED CLOTH
  – GREEK BORDER DESIGNS

NOTICE HOW EVEN THE NEGATIVE SHAPES TAKE ON GREEK PROPERTIES
LIKE A GREEK VASE

NOTICE THE TREES

GREEK POTTERY ART IS EXCELLENT REFERENCE FOR BACKGROUNDS

BRVCE ZICK

ABOVE AND OPPOSITE PAGE: *Sue Nichols created production design guides to help the artists integrate a widely varied set of influences. Bruce Zick's developmental work* (ABOVE), *Greek shapes* (OPPOSITE TOP), *and Gerald Scarfe's line* (OPPOSITE BOTTOM).

BELOW: *Concept art of Meg by Sue Nichols.*

The books remain with the animators, their assistants and the cleanup artists as ready reference guides during the long period of production. Sometimes basic designs can get lost; in *Beauty and the Beast*, Nichols observes, "we had over 200 years of costuming."

She reasons: "When you're in the fever of production, you don't have time to stop and go to a library and do research. This way, it's already been researched for you. We have the key elements of the book on a board downstairs in front of the pod (the nerve center for *Hercules*). So even if you don't have time to go through the book, at least it's hanging there and can be seen every day and be remembered."

She is impressed by how easily Scarfe's style adapts to animation:

"Gerald has a very free-flowing calligraphic arm. One of the best things about his style is that it is very expressive. There's a lot of animation and movement and caricature in his art. There is so much gesture and animation in just one of his drawings that it's very inspirational.

"But because it is such a free-flowing style, it needs to be tightened for production purposes so that several people—not only the key animator but all his or her assistants and the key cleanup person and their assistants—can draw that exact same drawing. There is the danger that it might be tightened up to a point where it may lose that freeness that Gerald has.

"Up to now we've been very structure-oriented," says Nichols. "When a character moved, that form might squash and stretch, but it wouldn't exaggerate to the point where it would lose form. This is the first time we've found incredibly graphic guideposts where the style is focusing more on gesture and movement, rather than just technical form and building a character."

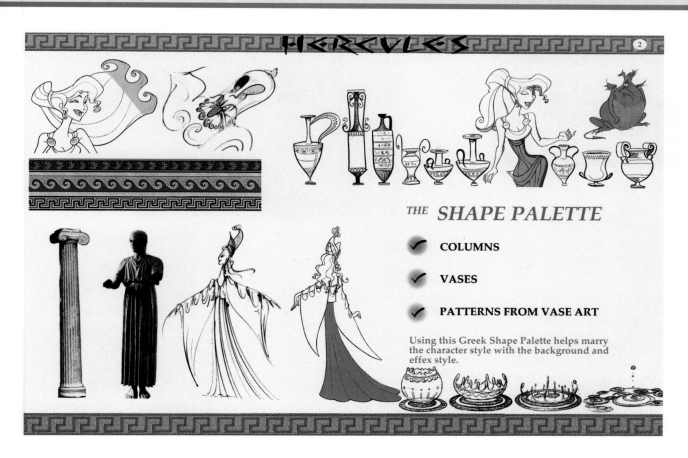

THE SHAPE PALETTE

✓ **COLUMNS**

✓ **VASES**

✓ **PATTERNS FROM VASE ART**

Using this Greek Shape Palette helps marry the character style with the background and effex style.

the SCARFE LINE :

You're standing in front a four foot piece of paper armed with pen and ink. You use your entire arm to lay down a powerful swoop causing your line to elegantly vary from thick to thin.

key word :

SWOOP !

Sometimes when you pick up your pen you cap your line with a small hook.

Or in mid - swoop you reverse direction suddenly, aggressively.

This **swoop with a sudden reversal** is a key Scarfe line !

the "S" curve

Do not let your "S" curve get soft and mushy.

Avoid using equal weights

Keep your "S" curve powerful by varying weights from large to small.

the Scarfe scallop

an aggressive line

not soft and passive

This large to small "S" curve creates a tapering in the shapes ...

necks are thick at their base and taper up to the chin

limbs tend to taper (unless it's against character)

This helps our calligraphic look !

ABOVE: *Writers Don McEnery and Bob Shaw.*

RIGHT: *A page from the illustrated script. Art by Andy Gaskill and Hans Bacher.*

BELOW: *Storyboard art of Hercules and the trapped boys by Kirk Hanson.*

BOY #1 (O.S.)
⟨HE⟩LP! CAN ANYONE...

BOY #1:   ...HEAR US?
BOY #2:   ...WE'RE IN HERE!
BOY #1:   GET US OUT!

BOY #1
(COUGH) WE'RE SUFFOCATING!

BOY #1 (O.S.)   SOMEBODY CALL IXII!
BOY #2 (O.S.)   HUR⟨RY⟩!

Script: Irene Mecchi, Don McEnery, Bob Shaw

In live-action movies, script writing generally is done by one person or two working as a team. While it is often considered a sign of a problem picture when multiple writers are called in to work on a live action film, the opposite is true in animated features. In this medium, script writing is an ongoing process involving many people over long periods of time.

For *Hercules,* the script began with Joe Haidar's page-and-a-half presentation. When Ron Clements and John Musker came aboard as directors, they wrote their own script, prompting the go-ahead for the production. Storyboard artists contributed, and while Musker and Clements continued making additions, three more writers—Irene Mecchi, Don McEnery, and Bob Shaw—were added to the mix.

"This is a gigantic collaborative process," says Shaw. "There is a lot to cull from. The storyboard people come in with their ideas. You can take your idea and their idea. It's great."

HADES — LADIES... HAH!

HADES I AM SO SORRY THAT I'M...
ATROPOS LATE!

ATROPOS We KNEW YOU WOULD BE...

HADES RIGHT! WELL, YOU'RE THE FATES.

ATROPOS WE KNOW EVERYTHING.

PAST...

CLOTHO PRE-...

CLOTHO ...-SENT...

LACHESIS ...AND...

LACHESIS ...FUTURE...

ATROPOS INDOOR PLUMBING, IT'S GONNA BE BIG.

HADES GREAT... ANYWAY...

Mecchi, McEnery, and Shaw often meet with the directors, producer, and storyboard artists, and appear at recording sessions with the actors, especially when comedy is involved.

"Being at a recording session is like a writing session for us," remarks Shaw. "You sit in the booth, and you have the opportunity to ad lib over and over. The directors, who are also in the booth, take the funny lines that you've said and distribute them to the actors."

The actors first deliver the lines as written, and then changes can be made. Musker and Clements are inclined to allow the actors to ad lib, especially after Robin Williams' inspired improvisation as the Genie in *Aladdin*.

A San Franciscan who studied theater and literature at the University of California at Berkeley, Irene Mecchi worked in theater and children's television before moving into sitcom writing. She was hired to write a film for Disney Educational Productions that was being made at Feature Animation, "Recycle Rex." Then she was assigned to a project called *King of the Jungle* "that nobody wanted to work on." She asked for a script and was told there wasn't one. Her work earned her co-writing credit on the film, which was renamed *The Lion King*.

Both McEnery and Shaw came from sitcom backgrounds via standup comedy. They decided to work together as writers and found success in television comedy, most notably *Seinfeld*.

"The Disney people knew our TV work, and they wanted funny people, since Musker and Clements are comedy guys," says Shaw. "But our work is not only comedy; it's also structural."

ABOVE: *Storyboard art of Hades and the three Fates by Barry Johnson.*

BELOW: *Writer Irene Mecchi.*

"I think the difference for a writer is that in animated films you look better because you get more drafts," says Irene Mecchi. "Rehearsals are in front of you on the storyboard. We continue to work with the material through production, and it gets redrawn and re-recorded. When you see the story reels, it's like seeing a play rehearsed from beginning to end. "People ask me, 'Don't you get frustrated doing it over and over again?' I say no, because I hope it keeps getting better and better."

ABOVE: *Storyboard art by Barry Johnson.*

BELOW: *Head of Story Barry Johnson with story art of the Muses.*

Story: Barry Johnson

A complex production like *Hercules* involving a few hundred artists needs someone to keep it in sync. That's the responsibility of Barry Johnson, who heads the story department.

"It's my job to coordinate all the story artists as they get their assignments and get started on their specific sequences," he explains. "I become the liaison between the directors and all the artists, just to make sure that everyone's on track.

"When people start looking at their scenes in particular, they start losing the big picture. So it's my job to keep the big picture—this sequence is going to affect someone else's sequence. I just try to keep everyone informed."

Johnson keeps abreast of the latest activities. If dialogue or songs have been changed, if an actor gave a different reading from what had been planned, Johnson does "fixes." That means drawing new storyboards or sketches to visualize the new material. He remains in contact with the directors and producer, attends story meetings and reviews reels to keep up with the film's progress.

A native of Sioux City, Iowa, Johnson studied English and psychology at the University of South Dakota. He had always enjoyed drawing, and came west to study animation at CalArts. After working at small animation houses and for the television series *Family Dog*, he signed on with Disney. His first assignment: storyboard artist on *The Lion King*.

As head of story for *Hercules*, Johnson directs a staff of a dozen artists. "They never tire of their work," Johnson says, "because the characters are so uniquely bizarre and the settings colorfully varied—everything from the Underworld to Mount Olympus."

SO, DID THEY GIVE YOU A...

MEG

...NAME, ALONG WITH ALL...

... THOSE RIPPLING PECTORALS?

What remains of the age-old Greek myths?

"Quite a bit, actually," Johnson replies. "I think Ron and John's approach, when they were initially writing the script, was that a lot of the myths would be either insinuated in this movie or depicted. For instance, the twelve labors of Hercules. They're not really a big story point. They might be treated in the context of a song.

"We tried to keep faithful to the Greek mythology, at the same time putting our twist on it. We're not inventing a lot of things that are totally different from the Greek. We're just interpreting it differently."

Much of the story department's work consists of reworking scenes, and trying to find new gags to enliven the action.

"In all the other divisions, people are a little bit separated," Johnson observes. "They're working with the directors, but they still have to go away and do their scenes. In the story department, we're constantly doing gags and showing them to the people we see all day long. We'll get up and pitch in front of everyone to get the group's reaction and take the criticism or take the compliments. 'Is this funny?' 'You like this?' It's unique."

PHIL LISTEN TO me kid, I've seen 'em all ...

PHIL ... And I am telling you, and this is the honest to Zeus truth...

PHIL You've got something I never seen before.

ABOVE: *Before the animation process begins, a story reel integrating the available images is created and reworked to establish the pacing of the scenes. These color keys by Colin Stimpson illustrate some editorial characteristics of* Hercules, *such as quick-cuts and close-ups.*

Editing: Tom Finan

Motion picture editing is defined in the *Film Encyclopedia* as "the process of selecting, assembling and arranging motion picture shots and corresponding sound tracks in coherent sequence and flowing continuity."

But is there a difference in editing animated features? "Decidedly," says Tom Finan. He spent the first 20 years of his career editing live-action films, coming to animation on *The Lion King*.

"At the end of *The Lion King* I stepped back and took a look," he says. "The truth is that I bring the same skills and the same tools to animation that I did in live action. It all amounts to storytelling. That's what an editor does.

"The editing room has often been called 'home of the final rewrite.' What is said on the script pages is not necessarily what is said when we cut negative on it. In animation it goes much farther than that.

"What I like about it is that I'm not only the 'home of the final rewrite,' I'm also involved with the initial writing. When I was in live action, I usually came on the film the first day of shooting, or a week before that. I wasn't involved in any prep, story meetings or the writing of the script.

"*Hercules* is different. When I came on, there was a bit of a script, more like a draft. It has changed considerably, and I am involved. Not just in the moving picture end of it, but in the actual words. That's nice. I enjoy it."

Another thing Finan enjoys about animation is the ability to use four or five different takes to build the meaning of a single sentence. Once the editing of a scene is done, the animators take over.

Such editing would be impossible in live action, where the editor is presented completed takes, with dialogue. To break up a sentence in live action would make it too "cutty," Finan explains.

MEG   Do you have any problems with things like...

MEG   ...this
HERC UUUHH   15·25A

MEG   Weak ankles, I mean.

ABOVE: *Dialogue like this repartee between Hercules and Meg (storyboard art by Kaan Kalyon) requires some finessing. The film's editor may pull pieces from multiple voice tracks in order to create a version that captures just the right tone, timing, and temperament.*

ABOVE LEFT: *Producer Alice Dewey, Directors Ron Clements and John Musker, and Editor Tom Finan edit* Hercules *on the AVID.*

BELOW: *Susan Egan gives voice to the witty and seductive Meg.*

Finan and his crew do their jobs in the early stages of production, working from story sketches. Each scene and cut is timed down to seconds. Pacing has to be flexible enough for animation's needs, but the first cut is a good indication of how the directors feel things will play. Jeff Jones, an associate editor, adds sound effects to help dramatize the sketches, and Earl Ghaffari puts in temporary background music from pre-recorded sources.

"The AVID, an electronic editing machine which edits digitized film in a computer, has made the life of an editor much easier than it was before when film was transferred to tape," observes Finan, "but it's hard on assistants. A lot of material goes into it. The main advantage is that it gives you the opportunity to make more choices, different versions."

After rough animation is completed and assembled, another assessment is made: "Is this shot needed?" "Do we need something else here?" It is symptomatic that the movie starts to grow as animation pours in; often the animator needs more screen time to complete a movement than the early edit with story sketches indicated. With the film now stretching six or seven minutes longer than the allotted 82 minutes, cuts must be made.

Tom Finan at 18 was employed as a carpenter in the San Fernando Valley when a shoulder injury prevented him from working. He met a film editor who suggested editing would be good work for him. He took a job as apprentice at CBS *Sports*, knowing nothing about the film business, much less editing. He worked his way up through television and features as one of the editors on *Platoon*, *Salvador* and other films.

"Animation feature editing is not taken as seriously as live-action editing," Finan declares. "It is assumed that the animators draw it up, and all I do is cut off the slates and build it. People don't realize that I cut the show first.

"I believe that *The Lion King* had 187,000 feet of recorded dialogue. The final product went out at about 8,000 feet. There are tremendous choices that are made in editorial."

The animated film, Rasoul Azadani observes, is a bombardment of images—1,500 scenes in 70 minutes, with animation on top of it. If those scenes are busy and confusing, the viewer gets lost. The scenes have to be designed to deliver information fast.

"That's what the good painters did," Azadani remarks. "Like Edward Hopper. If you look at his work, first it's abstract: a bunch of shapes, dark, light. Then you see a building. He's really a designer and not just painting a building.

"I thought 'Wow!—this is a great way to approach animation.' I think we're getting closer to this kind of design, and I hope we continue to move forward in this direction."

ABOVE: Layout Supervisor Rasoul Azadani.

TOP RIGHT: The members of the layout department create workbook pages that act as road maps, leading the animators and background artists through the frames and camera angles of a scene. This workbook page by Vincent Massey calls for the camera to pull back as the Cyclops snatches Hercules up in his giant fist.

BELOW: Concept art of Mt. Olympus by Rasoul Azadani.

PULL BACK as the Cyclops raises up with Hercules in his fist.

Meg (O.S.): I...I...I NEED YOU.

Layout: Rasoul Azadani

When Rasoul Azadani was an 8-year-old boy in Isfahan, Iran, his father took him to a screening of Bambi at a local theater. Young Rasoul was overwhelmed by what he saw. "I really want to work with those people, that's what I want to do," he told his dubious father.

The young man pursued his goal. He studied at the Academy of Art and worked in Iranian animation, which was created principally for educational purposes. In 1978 he emigrated to America, though his only knowledge of the language and culture was derived from movies.

Slowly he learned to speak English and to adjust to American ways, so foreign to what he had known in Iran. He attended Los Angeles City College and then was admitted to CalArts. After three years, he was hired by Disney to work on layout for The Great Mouse Detective.

"I always loved layout, because it utilized what I was trained for, which was fine art," he says. "Also I was interested in filmmaking, especially films of the 1940s by Elia Kazan and others.

"When I came here, I felt the animation was not as strong as when they were making Cinderella and Alice in Wonderland. I said something is missing, I think it is in approaching it as an art, rather than as a cartoon. The Disney film is more like character animation, dealing with the reality of life and what nature is. We have to push it and caricature it."

The walls of Azadani's office are lined with sketches, charts and photographs spilling out into the hallway. Included are "value charts" of the 21 major sequences

THIS PAGE: *The line layout is the blueprint for the scene's composition. The light design adds a layer of complexity by pinpointing the source of light—the layout artist dictates where light and shadow appear. The tonal layout establishes the brightness and contrast. The combination of these various layers determines the mood of the scene. These layouts provide the background artist with a frame of reference from which to paint the background.*

LEFT: *This line layout of the Hydra canyon by Denise Klitsie provides a stage for the battle between Hercules and the Hydra.*

RIGHT: *The sharp, angular shapes created in this light design by Rasoul Azadani provide a hostile texture for the Hydra canyon. Enclosing the scene, the canyon walls extend off the page.*

LEFT: *This tonal layout by Denise Klitsie provides the dim atmosphere for the staging of the dramatic fight between Hercules and the Hydra.*

ABOVE: *This preproduction layout of Meg's garden by Lissa Ainley fuses Greek elements such as columns and drapery forms with Scarfe's swoops and S-curves, and Bruce Zick's waves and swirls.*

OPPOSITE ABOVE: *Tonal layout of the sarcophagus overlooking the amphitheater by Yong Zhong.*

OPPOSITE BELOW: *Background painting of the sarcophagus by Sunny Apinchapong-Yang.*

of *Hercules*. They indicate the time of day and the emotion of the sequence. He points out several: in the museum, low key with spotlights; then Olympus, high key with clouds and light; the Underworld, dark and forbidding. The charts are done in white and shades of gray.

"The masters—Rembrandt, N.C. Wyeth and others—they really did the same thing," says Azadani. "They planned the toners, they put dark and light on it. We thought if they can plan one sequence, which is a canvas, we can do the whole film.

"You can see how the whole film cuts together. So if you have a low-key sequence and you cut to the next one, it's nice to have a higher key. It makes a more dynamic change from sequence to sequence. It depends on the story."

In planning the layout, Azadani regularly consults the masters, and he keeps books at hand for ready reference. He especially admires Gustave Doré, the French painter and illustrator. Other favorites: Goya for dynamics, Rembrandt for lighting, Hopper for shape and contrast of dark and light. He also likes the simplicity of Japanese artists like Hokusai and Hiroshige.

Azadani's layout depicts the cuts and camera angles of a sequence, but he doesn't expect it to be followed precisely—"I have the feeling that such things should evolve through the process; if we decide everything here, it's like putting a handcuff on the artist's hand and saying, 'That's it!'"

During the trip to Greece and Turkey, Azadani took a large number of photographs, many of which are on his walls. He also revisited Iran, where he reminisced with his father about their long-ago viewing of *Bambi*.

"Do you remember that I said I really wanted to work with the people who made *Bambi*?" he asked. "Believe it or not, I got to work with one of them who was still at the Studio. His name was Eric Larson."

Backgrounds: Tom Cardone

When Walt Disney introduced the multiplane camera with *The Old Mill* in 1937, it represented a giant step forward in the production of animation backgrounds. At last, depth could be achieved in backgrounds, which had been flat since the days of Emile Cohl and Winsor McCay.

The computer age marked another revolution in the creation of backgrounds. Computer graphics were first employed at Disney in *The Black Cauldron*. *The Rescuers Down Under*, the first film to use the new Computer Animation Production System (CAPS), benefited from a wider range of color and more fluid movement of the camera. The film was the first assignment at the Studio for Tom Cardone.

The New York native studied at the New York Institute of Technology, which had a laboratory that pioneered computer software. Cardone was working with computer painting at the same time Disney decided to convert to a new CAPS. He came to the Studio and contributed to the painting of *The Rescuers Down Under*, then moved into the background department.

"Backgrounds are still painted by hand. We use the computer paint program to adjust and manipulate paintings after they are scanned into CAPS. For example, if a painting needs to be extended we can do it in the system. If the change was made by hand, it would involve four people in two departments and a few days to make its way through. Now we can do it in 45 minutes."

ABOVE: *The monochromatic gray-blue of the Underworld can be seen in this background art by Tom Cardone (based on a drawing by Bruce Zick). Devoid of color, the Underworld's gloomy look is very distinct from that of either Earth or Olympus.*

"We use the computer as an aid, mostly to enhance and strengthen images. Plus, once an image is set, you can adjust it on the monitor to exactly what you want. When you do it by hand, you're still taking that chance: 'I think this is dark enough.' But you never know, because it changes. With the computer we can tweak things."

Cardone's first trip to Europe was the journey to Greece and Turkey with the other *Hercules* department heads. He was dazzled by the sights and impressed with how remote the Turkish ruins were—"We had to climb a mountain to get there; they were in the middle of nowhere, no tour buses, no admission charge, just a shepherd and a flock of sheep."

He produced numerous color keys—combinations of colors that would fit a scene—on the trip, capturing different shades on paper the size of a large postage stamp. He explains, "I work small so that I focus more on color relationships rather than detail. I can also make adjustments relatively quickly as the color is being thought out. Then we can approach the finished piece with more confidence."

Cardone's color approach for Thebes emerged as a variant of Manhattan. His first effort was considered too "cheery" for a city past its prime. So he made the cityscape moody, overcast, verging on rain. His source material is voluminous—

picture books of New York spill off his shelves. And for color inspiration: The Brandywine School, specifically N.C. Wyeth.

"He has a way of painting color: The grass isn't always green, the sky is not always blue," Cardone says admiringly. "On this film, we're trying to go for a bolder color statement with a simplified palette. It's actually more difficult to paint with a simple palette than to be more naturalistic.

"The directors wanted to go black and white with the Underworld," Cardone says. "We're getting a little blue into it as well. The Underworld is definitely a monochromatic statement."

When the characters are added, they will be color-keyed to the background, he adds. The art director keeps the background department informed of colors for the various figures.

"Hercules is still half-mortal, half-godlike," says Cardone, "and he glows a little bit. He won't glow throughout the film, but his skin tone will be more golden."

In the early stages, Cardone worked with a staff of four, with the department expanding to 29 after *The Hunchback of Notre Dame* finished production. *Hercules* is comprised of about 1,500 scenes, some of which use the same backgrounds. About 900 backgrounds, some requiring two weeks to paint, were created for the film.

ABOVE: *This background of the Centaur Woods by Natalie Franscioni-Karp utilizes simple, bold color to create a singular world.*

BELOW: *Tom Cardone drew this quick color key for reference during the Greece trip. It is shown here at the actual size at which it was painted.*

ABOVE: *Rough animation of Zeus by Lead Animator Tony DeRosa.*

ABOVE RIGHT: *Cleanup of Zeus by Merry Clingen, animation by Tony DeRosa.*

BELOW: *The Cleanup lead keys.* (FRONT ROW FROM LEFT TO RIGHT) *Kaaren Lundeen, Supervisor Nancy Kniep, Stephan Zupkas.* (MIDDLE ROW FROM LEFT TO RIGHT) *Bill Berg, Juliet Stroud-Duncan, Natasha Selfridge, Gail Frank, Ed Gutierrez.* (BACK ROW FROM LEFT TO RIGHT) *Marianne Tucker, Dan Tanaka, Terry Naughton, Merry Clingen, Kathy Bailey.*

Cleanup: Nancy Kniep

Cleanup is a misnomer for what has been an essential element of the animation process from its historical beginnings. "It sounds janitorial," Nancy Kniep observes wryly. She is the supervisor of cleanup for *Hercules*.

During the making of *Beauty and the Beast*, a contest was conducted to rename the cleanup department. It ended in failure; no one could suggest a suitable substitute.

What exactly is the function of cleanup?

"Cleanup is responsible for keeping the character looking consistent throughout the whole film," Kniep explains. "There are quite a few cleanup people working on one character. They will stay with that character throughout production and make sure it looks as if one person drew the same character all the way through.

"For instance, in the Hercules unit, headed up by Andreas Deja, there are other animators drawing Hercules under his supervision. The other animators may not draw the character exactly the same way he does. We have to make it look as if one animator drew all of them.

"In my department, the artists are very good draftsmen; they're very accurate, they can't make mistakes. The animators can make little mistakes. Some animators change the way they draw their characters constantly, they evolve during the picture. We have to make sure they don't.

"When we finish a scene, it has to be camera-ready. Any tiny little mistake comes back. We have to make sure every little buckle is where it belongs, every little hair in place."

As testimony to the importance of cleanup, it is the largest department on *Hercules* with more than 150 people, some of them 30-year Disney veterans. It's Kniep's job to keep them all happy, match each with the right characters and animators and crews so the job can be done with a degree of harmony. She knows all their talents and foibles. Some artists are proficient at drawing animals, others specialize in female characters.

Says Kniep, "They're in a learning curve on *Hercules* right now. They're learning the characters, and they're getting to know the animators. They'll get up to speed where drawing the characters with the correct style and precision will just come automatically."

Nancy Kniep was born in Burbank, not far from the Disney Studio. She studied art at California State University at Northridge and UCLA and worked at television animation studios, where cleanup is an unaffordable nicety. After three years in cleanup at Don Bluth Productions, she was hired at Disney and began on *Who Framed Roger Rabbit*. She became Co-cleanup Supervisor with Renée Holt-Bird on *Pocahontas*.

Cleanup relies on mutual relationships. "The animators trust us, and we trust them," she says. "We do what they want. But we do sometimes have to change a character if it is 'off-model.' Some Disney animators will draw their characters perfectly, there won't be much to do on their scenes other than to make sure that the character is solid throughout the whole scene. Other animators will need our help to put their characters on model. In all scenes we need to keep the volumes from changing and the dialogue strong and in sync. We watch that very closely.

"Even with the cleanest of animation, there may be some drawings that aren't camera-ready. We will have to check that all the proper arcs are there, the dialogue is solid, the hair isn't stiff but actually flows, and the drapery is moving properly. We make sure all that happens."

ABOVE LEFT AND RIGHT: *Cleanup of Pain by Stephan Zupkas, animation by James Lopez* (LEFT). *Zupkas' cleaned up lines are the very same lines that appear in the final frame of Pain wearing his new Hercules sandals* (RIGHT).

BELOW LEFT: *Cleanup of Hades by Bill Berg, animation by Nik Ranieri.*

BELOW: *Cleanup of Calliope by Merry Clingen, animation by Mike Show, lead animator for the Muses.*

ABOVE, ABOVE RIGHT, AND OPPOSITE ABOVE LEFT: *To blend the three-dimensional Hydra into a two-dimensional film, first a three-dimensional image is created on the computer. This image is then processed to remove all shading, and the computer adds inklines to create the effects of hand drawn art. Finally, lighting tones are added to the colored ink and paint levels to create the finished frame.*

BELOW: *Using morphing technology, a crib arises from the clouds in Olympus.*

Computer Generated Imagery: Roger Gould

When designing Olympus, home of the gods, the directors envisioned it not as a city in the clouds, but a city made of clouds. Achieving this effect proved a challenge.

"We wanted to create moving, living clouds that could magically transform at the whim of the gods," says Roger Gould. "We considered three-dimensional clouds, but felt they would stick out when combined with the traditional backgrounds. What we really wanted to create were animated background paintings." The solution was found in a device known as morphing.

"What morphing really is," Gould explains, "is a very fancy cross-dissolve, where one image turns into the next." Existing morph programs only allow morphing of two sets of moving pictures, such as a man turning into a werewolf.

"For our transformations, clouds billow and grow and then solidify into architecture, like columns and cribs. To animate through all these changes, we needed to create a series of painted keys and then morph among them. This required writing our own morph program.

"I thought this might work, but when we saw the first test we were all startled by how exciting it was to see paintings that moved! For example, in the scene where Hera creates Hercules's crib from the clouds we used just five paintings to create 132 frames of an animated background!"

Growing up in New York City, Roger Gould haunted retrospective movie theaters that showed early Disney and Warner Bros. shorts. He studied computer graphics at Brown University, convinced he had found the next frontier of animation. He also took courses in traditional animation at the Rhode Island School of Design, just in case he turned out to be wrong. Gould worked in advertising, music videos and Japanese theme parks before joining Disney in 1994 when *Hercules* was in its infancy.

Today he is well aware of the computer's limitations. "Three years ago there was an explosion. The computer imaging in *Jurassic Park* had a lot to do with it.

ABOVE: *CGI Supervisor Roger Gould.*

BELOW AND BELOW LEFT: *Color keys of Hercules battling the Hydra by Natalie Franscioni-Karp.*

Suddenly people saw things on the screen that they knew couldn't be real. For years we were trying to convince people that we could do something on the computer. Now we have to reassure people that we can't do everything."

The computer was a great aid in creating the action and movement that was desired in the Hydra sequence where Hercules confronts the beast. "The one thing that Ron and John wanted to do in this sequence was to push the scale of the Hydra. It is enormous. At one point in the battle you chop off one head and say, 'Hey, I'm doing great!' Of course it only gets worse, with more and more heads popping out. Hercules is forced on the defensive; he keeps slicing even though he knows it's a bad idea. He's flying around on Pegasus in this living jungle of Hydra heads and necks that attack him.

"The sequence's staging has the movement and depth that can be achieved with a helicopter camera—something that would be very difficult to work out on paper. We're taking advantage of that dimensionality of the computer to allow us to choreograph this battle. We're hoping the audience will be drawn into the space and feel the drama and the intensity of Hercules's struggle."

Content | Indigné | Mecontent | Furieux

ABOVE: *Effects concept drawing of Hades bursting into flames by Andy Gaskill.*

BELOW: *Effects concept drawing of a column of fire by Dan Chaika.*

BOTTOM: *Effects Supervisor Mauro Maressa.*

Special Effects: Mauro Maressa

"Nobody really knows what having effects does for a picture," comments Mauro Maressa. "If you did not have any effects, you'd notice. It would be like having a mermaid without water.

"What we add is an atmosphere, an environment. We put in tone and shadows, marry the characters to the background, along with all the other effects that we do: the water, the fire, the smoke. Usually it's peripheral. If we do our jobs correctly, you won't notice what we do."

Traditionally, effects have been fashioned by hand. Computers now play a role as well; in *Hercules* they help create Amphitryon's cart, the chariot taxi in Thebes, the gods' chariots, the tumbling of the columns in the Agora. In full production, the effects department will employ 40 artists, creating such wonders as the Titans who create tornadoes, lava and rock storms.

Maressa, who was born "at the tip of the toe" of Italy, came to the United States when he was eight, and later studied art at the New England School of Design and graduated with a teaching degree from the University of Massachusetts. Unable to find work as an illustrator, he taught school for three years. While honeymooning in California in 1978, he brought his portfolio to the Disney Studio and received encouragement. Six months later he quit teaching and entered the Disney training program.

Unfortunately for him, the Studio's animation was in a slump, and he was laid off three months later. He did stints at Hanna-Barbera, Ralph Bakshi, another spell at Disney, and then devised effects for live-action films such as *Poltergeist* II and *Aliens* III. He returned to Disney in 1993 to work on *The Lion King*. Among the effects he helped create was the 'Be Prepared' scene in which Scar leaps from one crumbling pillar to another, encountering dust, rocks and spewing steam. He spent some time on *Pocahontas*, then a year on *The Hunchback of Notre Dame*, during which he trained artists at Disney's Paris Studio.

Hercules, which is Maressa's first assignment as effects supervisor, is the most design-oriented film so far, thanks to Gerald Scarfe's original conceptions. "We're trying to keep true to that look in our effects," says Maressa. "We're dealing with three worlds: the Underworld of Hades; the real world; and Olympus.

HERCVLES

EFFECTS DESIGN

* DESIGN APPROACH FOR
SMALL SCALE "REAL
WORLD" SPLASHES

"Each of these worlds has its own look in the effects. The fire in the Underworld, a very barbed, twisted and tortured kind of environment. The smoke will follow along the same designs. In the real world, we have Greek keys in all our designs; water, smoke, and whatever we do will have that Greek flair. Olympus has its own look, though it is similar to the real world."

Maressa displays slides which demonstrate some of the work in progress:

"Here is the smoke which will be in Hades; it will be like ground swells. . . . With water, we use a lot of the keys from the shape of a vase. We begin with a realistic vase shape and then we put all the properties of water on it. This is the first stage of the Agora columns that will come crashing down in domino fashion. We'll be working with our technical directors, getting all the columns so they're solid. . . . We're well on our way."

ABOVE: *This page of* Hercules *effects design by James Mansfield shows the use of Greek forms of vases and columns in watersplashes.*

BELOW LEFT: *Once the drawings are completed, the people from the CAPs department provide the finishing touches.* (FROM LEFT TO RIGHT): *Robyn Roberts (Supervisor, Scanning), Hortensia Casagran (Supervisor, Painting/Final Check), J.R. Russell (Assistant Supervisor, Compositing), Chris Gee (Supervisor, Digital Film Print), Tom Baker (Supervisor, Scene Planning), Janet Bruce (Supervisor, Animation Check), Karen Comella (Supervisor, Color Models).*

BELOW: Hades *in his fury.*

CHAPTER ELEVEN
ANIMATING HERCULES

ABOVE: *Underworld Lead Animators* (LEFT TO RIGHT): *Nik Ranieri* (Hades), *Brian Ferguson* (Panic), *Nancy Beiman* (The Three Fates) *and James Lopez* (Pain).

RIGHT: *Color key of the Underworld by Hans Bacher.*

BELOW: *Rough animation of Hades by Lead Animator Nik Ranieri.*

PRECEDING SPREAD: *Pre-production key of Earth by Tom Cardone* (SPREAD). *Final animation of Meg* (INSET).

U N D E R W O R L D

Hades: Nik Ranieri

Nik Ranieri doesn't lack for inspiration around the table where he animates Hades. He has Gerald Scarfe's sketches of the lord of the Underworld, his hair flaming like a jet afterburner. He also has 16 snapshots of James Woods, the voice of Hades.

"At a recording session I asked Woods if I could take photos of him in different poses," Ranieri recalls. "He said sure, and we went outside the recording studio. I was like a photographer: 'Work with me. . . . Give me anger. . . . Give me sadness.' He was very accommodating."

Nearby is the animator's ancient tool: the mirror. Down through the years animators have relied on their own images to inspire a sneer, a grin, a lift of the eyebrow. "It's helpful with dialogue and expressions, especially with Hades," he admits. "Some mornings I come in and feel like Hades. Mostly Monday mornings."

Nik Ranieri's natural talent for cartooning led him to Sheridan College, "the CalArts of Canada," where many of Disney's Canadian émigrés were schooled. He worked on shorts and commercials in Toronto and Montreal, many of them combining animation with live action. Traveling to England, he applied for work on *Who Framed Roger Rabbit*, and his experience made him a natural for the film. At Disney in Burbank he worked on many characters, notably the irrepressible Lumiere in *Beauty and the Beast*.

Ranieri envisions Hades as a different kind of Disney villain:

"He starts out being somewhat likable. He's cracking jokes, making fun. Then you realize after a while that it's all surface. He's not a nice guy. By the end of the film you realize he gets what he deserves."

Ranieri envisions Hades as not pure evil—"more of a smooth talker, a Hollywood agent; those types of guys can be the scariest."

Hades may start out like one of those smooth-talking guys who insist "Let's do lunch," but he ends up as something far different. The effects department contributes to his menace. He moves in a half-walking, half-floating manner, the hem of his coat disappearing in a billow of smoke. His hair glows like a gas flame, cool and blue. During periods of rage, the flame intensifies to a bright red.

"Usually in a Disney film you start out by saying, 'This guy's a jerk, he's not a nice guy.' We turn the tables a bit and start out with him more sympathetic. The contrast is good for the character."

Hades became a villain of convenience for Disney's *Hercules*. In the original Greek myth, Hera is the evil force. For plot purposes, she became a loving figure. Hades, ruler of the dead in the Underworld, was enlisted as villain.

"The idea is not necessarily to tell Greek mythology in its purest form," Ranieri reasons, "as much as it is to convey a theme. The theme of the film is: What does it mean to be a true hero?"

ABOVE: *James Woods crafts the voice for the smooth-talking* Hades.

LEFT: *Rough animation of* Hades *by Nik Ranieri.*

BELOW LEFT: Hades *eating worms.*

BELOW: *Rough animation of the three Fates by Lead Animator Nancy Beiman.*

ABOVE: *Rough animation of Pain by Lead Animator James Lopez.*

ABOVE RIGHT: *Concept art of Pain and Panic by James Lopez.*

BELOW RIGHT: *Rough animation of Panic by Lead Animator Brian Ferguson.*

BELOW: *Panic slurps his Hercules soda.*

Pain and Panic: James Lopez and Brian Ferguson

Brian Ferguson and James Lopez work in adjoining offices at the western end of the building, and their laughter is often heard by their colleagues. "When I was designing Panic, I started with his eyes, trying to show him in a state of real fear," comments Ferguson. "The designs weren't working; he looked more like a worried character, rather than one in panic. Then I came up with a design that had him really cowering, with an elongated head. That's basically what he is now."

Ferguson's early years took him from Venezuela to Boston and finally to western Canada, where he graduated with a degree in zoology from the University of Alberta. He studied animation at Sheridan College and worked on an animation feature in New York. Disney offered Ferguson a job which he quickly accepted.

James Lopez hails from the Southern California town of Cerritos and started drawing at the age of three and a half. He enrolled at CalArts in 1988. He came to Disney to assist on *The Lion King* and later on *Pocahontas*. Like Ferguson, he has his first assignment as supervising animator with *Hercules*.

Both Lopez and Ferguson find inspiration in the voices of Bobcat Goldthwait (Pain) and Matt Frewer (Panic). "Just listening to the voices of Bob and Matt automatically gives you a picture— 'Oh, that's the way to do it!'"

During the film, Hades' nasty little operatives transmogrify into worms, snakes, rabbits, gophers, and small boys, even a flirty female winged horse to lure Pegasus. "That's the difficult part: designing the characters these two guys turn into," comments Lopez. "Designing Pain was a whole lot easier. When I tried to design a bunny rabbit, the directors said, 'Make it really cute, a typical Disney bunny rabbit.' Well, I went to the archives and came up with a design. 'It's not cute enough,' the directors said. I struggled a long time with it."

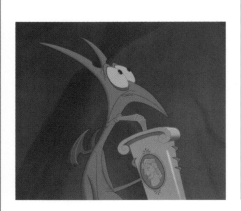

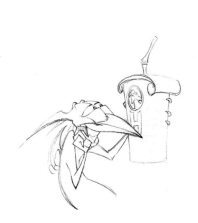

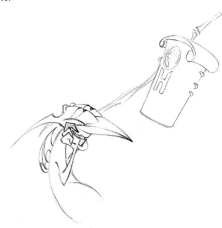

Earth

Hercules: Andreas Deja

When Andreas Deja was an art student in Dusseldorf, West Germany, his mother wouldn't allow him to attend life drawing classes. "I don't want you looking at those naked bodies," she declared. Only when her son turned 16 did she permit him to attend such classes. The experience helped him to animate the world's most legendary athlete.

Deja is bringing a different kind of drawing to the depiction of Hercules's musculature. "Normally we don't do lines within the body," he explains. "If we animate a male character, we would only draw the muscles from the outside, defining the bicep by the outline. The Greek paintings had lines within the arm. That hasn't been done in animation before because it might look too harsh and too graphic. But here it seems to work with the style."

Deja was born in Gdansk in communist Poland, and his family escaped to West Germany when he was only a year old. He tells of watching "The Wonderful World of Disney" on television and seeing Walt Disney appear to speak fluent German. When he was ten, seeing *The Jungle Book* in a theater inspired him to pen a letter to the Disney Studio inquiring how to become an animator. A form letter suggested that he not try to imitate Disney characters but develop his own skills.

After his army training, Deja sent drawings to Eric Larson, who was impressed with the young man's work. A meeting was arranged in Germany, and in 1980 Deja came to the Studio to train. Eight weeks later he was hired full-time.

ABOVE: *Color key of Centaur Woods by Tom Cardone.*

BELOW: *Rough animation of Hercules by Lead Animator Andreas Deja.*

ABOVE: *Tate Donovan gives voice to Hercules.*

ABOVE RIGHT: *Animation of Meg by Ken Duncan, cleanup by Marianne Tucker. Animation of Hercules by Andreas Deja, cleanup by Dan Tanaka.*

BELOW RIGHT: *Rough animation of Nessus by Lead Animator Chris Bailey.*

BELOW: *An angry Hercules.*

His assignments escalated in importance: King Triton in *The Little Mermaid*, Mickey Mouse in *The Prince and the Pauper*, Gaston in *Beauty and the Beast*, Jafar in *Aladdin*, Scar in *The Lion King*. Now, the title character in *Hercules*.

"You don't want to make him an Arnold Schwarzenegger," Deja observes. "You have to find out who he is. In the beginning he is very innocent, very naive. So it gives you a nice contrast to the strength that he has."

Deja began with the Scarfe conception of Hercules, then interpreted it himself, searching for the element that the character would need for storytelling purposes. After several tries, he arrived at the solution: Return to the Greek tradition.

"That means the straight nose, pursed lips—almost cherubic, large eyes, a lidded look," he explains. "The classic style you find on Greek vases or drawings."

Deja also studied photographs of Olympic athletes. He rejected the appearance of weight lifters, with their short necks and bulging muscles. He preferred the look of swimmers, with their long necks and natural musculature.

Concerning Hercules's movement, Andreas Deja explains: "Toward the beginning of the movie, he really is a kid in a man's body, even though he is fully grown. He's still very inexperienced, hasn't traveled or met people. He sets out on this journey and meets Megara. He's very shy and insecure about how to react to this beautiful girl. He falls in love with her.

"He's also somebody who would show emotions right away; there's no reason for him to hide anything. He displays his emotions very clearly, very simply. Later on, when he runs into problems regarding misconceptions with what it means to become a hero, he gains experience and becomes more sure of himself. In the end he will take on Hades and fight him, which takes a lot of courage. He becomes a man, a more self-assured person."

ABOVE: Hercules looks on as Meg expresses her observations on the ways of the world (or men in particular).

LEFT: Concept drawing of Hercules by Andreas Deja.

ABOVE AND ABOVE RIGHT: *Rough animation of Baby Hercules by Lead Animator Randy Haycock.*

BELOW: *Character design drawing of young Hercules by Randy Haycock.*

Baby and Teenage Hercules: Randy Haycock

As a teenager in Grand Junction, Colorado, Randy Haycock dreamed of becoming a comic book artist. He even sent samples of his cartoons to Marvel Comics and received a printed reply: "We have no time to look at your work. . . . keep drawing."

Downcast, Randy decided to go see a movie, *Fantasia*, even though a cousin had called it "the most boring thing I've ever seen." Randy's decision afterward: "Comics are lowbrow; that's art!" As a student at Brigham Young University, he watched the new era of animation emerge with films like *Who Framed Roger Rabbit* and *The Little Mermaid*. Randy enrolled at CalArts, and his wife Angela worked to help support him.

Haycock arrived at Disney in 1992 and started as a rough in-betweener for Glen Keane on the character Aladdin. *Hercules* is his first stint as supervising animator. His assignment: Hercules as a baby and as an adolescent.

"When I first came on the picture, I had just come back from a little vacation after the birth of our first child, Riley Ann," says Haycock. "All I knew was that I was going to do Herc as a teenager. Ron and John told me,'We felt somebody should do the baby who has a baby. Would you like to do the baby, too?' I said, 'That's great!'"

Since his own baby was too young to use as a model, Haycock videotaped a friend's six-month-old, rented movies about babies, and did extensive research. By the time Haycock was ready to start animating Baby Hercules, Riley Ann was the perfect age to observe.

"This is where Herc gets his thick curly hair," the artist remarks, pointing to a photograph of his baby. "More than that, his mannerisms come right off things I've picked up from her. I find that the real appeal is not the slapstick things that you might do, but that he does everything like a baby does. People identify him with a real baby, even though he's more caricatured."

The inspiration for the adolescent Hercules came from Randy Haycock himself.

"When I was a teenager in high school, I was six feet tall and weighed 140 pounds," he recalls. "I was too tall and skinny for my age, and I was a lousy athlete. At home I broke just about everything that was breakable."

Young Hercules has the big hands and big feet that Haycock remembers having. "His lack of coordination is something that parents are going to see in their teenagers and teenagers are going to see in themselves and identify with him more. I think that adds to his appeal, that he can be humorous sometimes."

Philoctetes: Eric Goldberg

Eric Goldberg has been cartooning all his life. Growing up in New Jersey, he delighted his friends with his drawings. After studying illustration at Pratt Institute in Brooklyn, he connected with Richard Williams, who was making *Raggedy Ann and Andy* in New York while operating a commercial studio in London. Goldberg moved to Williams' London headquarters, worked several years in commercials and television, then opened Pizazz Pictures with two partners.

"We lasted six years until someone at Disney called and said, 'Ready to jump ship yet?'" he recalls. Although his company was busy making commercials, Goldberg decided it was time to make a move. He saw how animation was enjoying a renaissance in his native country with *The Little Mermaid*, *Who Framed Roger Rabbit*, "The Simpsons," and others.

Goldberg started at the top: as supervising animator on the Genie in *Aladdin*. Next, he and Mike Gabriel directed *Pocahontas*. He missed animating, and he returned to it with Phil in *Hercules*.

"Phil is basically your fight trainer-mentor-Yoda figure," Goldberg analyzes. "He's the guy who has trained all the heroes, and they all flaked out on him. They all had great potential, but they could never pull out that something extra. Phil says, 'Achilles! He had the moves! He had the physique! But that fershlugginah heel of his!'" Goldberg laughs loudly, as he does throughout the conversation. Here is an artist who obviously savors his work.

Goldberg's sketches of Phil reveal a wide range of expressions. That's his favorite style and why he enjoys working with John Musker and Ron Clements. He finds their films are more "cartoony," in contrast to more serious works such as *Pocahontas* and *The Hunchback of Notre Dame*.

"With a character like Phil, you can push his expressions," observes Goldberg. "He's a very bombastic guy with a very low boiling point. And he also has a lascivious side, as befits a satyr."

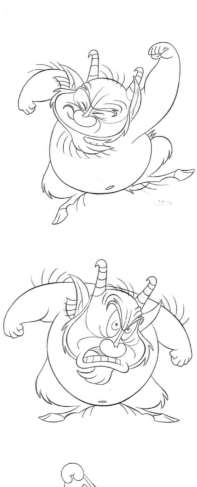

ABOVE: *Animation by Lead Animator Eric Goldberg, cleanup of Phil by Ed Gutierrez.*

ABOVE LEFT: *Phil coaches Hercules as he battles Nessus.*

ABOVE: *Danny DeVito provides the voice for Phil.*

RIGHT: *Phil flirts with Meg.*

BELOW: *Rough animation of Hercules and Phil by Eric Goldberg.*

In designing Phil, Goldberg retained the fluidity and the shape orientation of Gerald Scarfe's work and the boldness of caricature, adding that indefinable quality called "Disney appeal." The casting of Danny DeVito as the voice of Phil brought his unique personality to the character.

At one point Goldberg tried a literal caricature of DeVito with horns. Musker and Clements vetoed it. DeVito remained a strong influence on Phil, and Goldberg also borrowed from classic characters of Disney's past, notably the face construction of Ward Kimball's Bacchus in *Fantasia* and the curmudgeonly nature of Grumpy in *Snow White and the Seven Dwarfs*.

Phil is apathetic and listless in the beginning—except when he's chasing nymphs. He rejects Hercules's pleas to be his trainer, having been disappointed too many times by his hero trainees. But once he gets started he's a whirlwind.

"That's one thing that's kind of nice about the character," Goldberg comments. "You can get a heckuva lot of bombast out of him when he boils over and gets angry. But ultimately he's got a lot of pain in him, and he's trying to work that through. Hercules helps him deal with it."

As for Phil's shape, Goldberg explains: "He's short, he's bald, he's overweight. I can relate."

Megara: Ken Duncan

Ken Duncan works surrounded by visions of Meg. Duncan paints a word picture of the character he will live with for a year and a half: "She's very independent, sort of a street-wise girl. She's been through a lot in her life; she's probably been betrayed by people in her past. Meg's got a very sarcastic way of working with people, protective of herself. She doesn't get too close to anybody. In the film she learns to trust someone again, and that is Hercules.

"Meg was much too realistic at first for the directors and the style of the film," says Duncan. By degrees the final Meg emerged, sinewy, self-assured, alluring . . .

sassy! Now she fits in with the other characters of *Hercules* and the nature of the story.

"She's working for Hades, and at one time in the past she was used as a pawn in one of his deals. She doesn't really care for Hades; he's just the boss. At first, she's willing to double-cross Hercules to get her own freedom, but along the way she learns to care for him."

Like the directors, Ron Clements and John Musker, Duncan is inspired by the screwball comedies of the 1930s and 1940s and their stars. "They were very independent women with their own quick-witted minds," he observes.

Duncan demonstrates how he arrived at the figure of Meg. He draws the upper body and hips with the contours of a Greek vase; the waist and the torso take on the shape of a column. Then he slips a cassette into the VCR to demonstrate how Meg moves. It is a scene in which Hercules invites her on a ride with Pegasus. When the jealous Pegasus appears hostile, Meg comments, "I don't think your pinto likes me very much." The skirt and her hair move enticingly.

He displays another scene that takes place after Hercules rescues Meg from Nessus. Hercules fishes for her name, and she replies, "Megara. My friends call me Meg. Or at least they would if I had any friends." Admiring his torso, she adds, "Did they give you a name along with all those rippling pectorals?"

"To her, Hercules is just like any other man, someone to distrust." Duncan explains. "As the film goes along, she finds out he's basically a loner trying to deal with the fame of being Hercules. Meg's a loner, too, so they have more in common than she originally thought. So she opens up to him a bit more. This leads to some conflict between her instincts and her emotions."

Ken Duncan is another animator from north of the border. After college in Canada he went to Europe and worked in Paris on two animated films, then in London on television commercials. He also worked in Spain and Ireland. He came to Los Angeles and realized a longtime ambition by joining Disney in 1990. His first assignment: *The Rescuers Down Under*. He became a supervising animator on *Pocahontas*, assigned to the character of Thomas.

ABOVE: *Rough animation of Meg by Lead Animator Ken Duncan.*

BELOW: *This concept drawing by Ken Duncan exemplifies how Meg's creators pushed the concept of incorporating Greek forms to its limits. Greek vase shapes can be seen in her torso, hips, and head. The slim line of her body resembles a column, and her costume and hair reflect flowing drapery.*

ABOVE: *A surprised Pegasus after being denied a high-five by the smitten Hercules.*

RIGHT: *Rough Animation of Pegasus by Lead Animator Ellen Woodbury.*

BELOW: *Concept art of Baby Pegasus by Rick Maki.*

Pegasus: Ellen Woodbury

On a wall in Ellen Woodbury's office are pictures of the bronze horses atop St. Mark's Church in Venice, photos of horses on Greek vases, horses in rodeos, and the diving horses of the Atlantic City Steel Pier. There are also pictures of wide-winged birds, eagles, hawks, and more. All these help inspire Woodbury in her task of animating Pegasus.

Hollywood and Disney seemed far away from school in Corning, N.Y., but as a student at Syracuse University she set her goal to get there. She switched majors to art and film and took a course in animation. She enrolled at CalArts and joined Jules Engel's experimental program. Her thesis film helped win her a job at Disney, starting as assistant, animating hair and tails on *The Great Mouse Detective*. She first became a supervising animator working on Zazu in *The Lion King*.

Now she is charged with creating a different kind of animal, a flying horse.

"Gerald Scarfe's drawing of Pegasus was the starting point," she remarks. "Then I did research. See all this stuff on the walls? This is what I started with. I said, 'Let me learn about horses and Greek art and let me discover the different ways that people present horses.'"

She borrowed the brush-cut mane from a marble statue and found other sources of inspiration. "That's what Jules taught me: 'Look around at what's there; if things strike a chord, take them,'" she recalls.

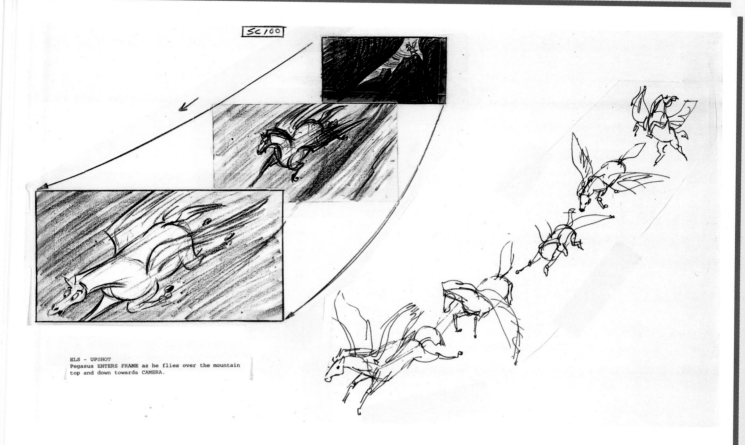

ELS - UPSHOT
Pegasus ENTERS FRAME as he flies over the mountain
top and down towards CAMERA.

Most of the characters she had animated were small. Now she was dealing with a horse. "It's a different way of thinking," she marvels. "You've got to think big. You've got to feel big. Pegasus's head is twice as long as Herc's head. It's just a matter of proportion, but you've got to think it, to feel it inside you. This is an enormous head."

But can a horse fly convincingly? That was her next big challenge. "I tried a walk, a trot, a canter, a gallop and then a leap into the air and finally, flying.

"Big birds of prey also have a feeling of weight; when you watch their weight, it's different from small birds. I think: I've got a big mass that I've got to lift. In the air big birds use the wind differently from small-bodied birds. That's how to get into it."

But Pegasus's majestic frame belies his nature. "He likes to rough-house and get dirty," says Woodbury. "He's a good-natured jock, with more looks than brains."

ABOVE: *Workbook drawing by Rasoul Azadani shows Pegasus flying down to earth to rescue Hercules from the Hydra.*

BELOW LEFT: *Concept art of Pegasus by Gerald Scarfe.*

ABOVE AND OPPOSITE ABOVE: *Animation of the battle between Hercules and the Hydra.*

BELOW: *Concept art of the thirty-headed Hydra by Howard Baker.*

OPPOSITE MIDDLE: *Rough animation of the Hydra by Oskar Urretabizkaia.*

OPPOSITE BELOW: *Concept art of Hercules battling the Hydra by Vance Gerry.*

Hydra: Oskar Urretabizkaia, Roger Gould, and CGI

The many-headed Hydra is the product of an ideal marriage of traditional animation and computer graphics imagery. Neither medium could successfully create the look alone. Oskar Urretabizkaia bears the responsibility of animating the fearsome beast. The CGI team headed by Roger Gould provides the writhing bodies and multiple heads for Hercules's mighty struggle.

Oskar Urretabizkaia started drawing in San Sebastian, a town in northern Spain's Basque country. He worked as an animator in Madrid, Paris, London and at George Lucas's Industrial Light and Magic in northern California, before coming to Disney to animate the Hydra.

"What I've been doing is trying to apply traditional animation skills to the computer," he remarks. "So I approached animating the Hydra just as I would approach animating on paper. I consider what a scene is trying to say and I draw thumbnails to explore the acting and expressions. But then, instead of animating on paper, I animate directly on the computer."

The Hydra sequence begins with one head, but each time Hercules slices one off, three more appear in its place. The multiple heads would be too time-consuming and tedious to accomplish in hand-drawn animation. Enter Roger Gould and his computer wizards.

On the first level of the Animation Building, Roger Gould sits before a screen on which a horrific Hydra with multiple heads snapping razor teeth stares back at him. The Hydra itself required six months to create, the battle sequence will take a year for Gould and his 13-member crew of animators and technical directors to animate. The result occupies approximately four minutes of screen time.

Early on, it was decided that the Disney Hydra would have 30 raging heads. "That was something nobody wanted to draw," says Gould. "But the computer is a

very patient artist. If we create one master head, the computer can multiply it on whatever scale we want."

The computer is also demanding, requiring three-dimensional models. Kent Melton converted the Hydra to a sculpture that captured all the style and ferocity of the hand-drawn version. The model was digitized into the computer, where it could be animated.

"The challenge for us was to take something that had to be built in a three-dimensional way," Gould remarks, "and then create animation and images and fit them into a film where everything else is being drawn by hand. The computer is good at moving rigid objects around. But when you're drawing, you can pull things out of shape and stretch them. That's not generally what you use the computer to do. So we have to teach the computer to let us be freer and looser with the model than we've ever been before."

Gould compares the method to working with a stop-motion puppet. Among the details requiring animation: the fins needed to bend upward, the eyes needed to open or squint, the jaw had to open and close. Virtually everything had to be stretched to achieve the looseness of the drawing. Gould switched his computer on to demonstrate the next step—losing dimensionality so the image would seem to be a hand-drawn character. Gould told the computer to paint the Hydra like a traditional cel. The Hydra's shading disappeared, an inkline was painted around it, and it looked two-dimensional. Some dimensionality was restored by having the computer draw the same type of shading that would normally be drawn by hand.

Urretabizkaia keeps a close eye on the process so that the animation and images created with the computer are as close to traditional as possible. He concludes, "We want the audience to watch the Hydra battle and be excited and entertained. Afterwards, when they say, 'I can't believe someone drew that!' we can say, 'We didn't.'"

Titans and the Cyclops: Dominique Monfery

Growing up in the north of France, Dominique Monfery became fascinated with comics and movies. When he saw *The Jungle Book*, his destiny was assured: he would become an animator. After two years of study in Paris, he was hired by a French television company. In 1989, he joined Disney animation in Paris, beginning as a cleanup artist. Soon he was animating, and he came to Burbank twice, first for *The Runaway Brain* and then for *The Hunchback of Notre Dame*.

His obvious talent led John Musker and Ron Clements to cast Monfery as animator for the Titans.

"Ron and John sent me the conceptual drawings, and then I made my own interpretation," says Monfery, speaking from the Paris studio.

"The perspective is a challenge, because Hercules only comes up to the Titans' ankles. I made drawings from above and from below so we could see how it would look."

The creation of the Cyclops and the Titans will occupy Monfery for a year. He works in Paris, far removed from production headquarters.

"Communication at first was difficult, but now we are used to it," Monfery remarks. "It seems normal. We have a conference room, we have video conferencing so we can see each other by television. Of course it would be easier if the directors were here, but we are in contact all the time."

ABOVE AND BELOW: *Concept art of the Cyclops by Lead Animator Dominique Monfery.*

ABOVE RIGHT: *Concept art of the Titans by Dominique Monfery.*

BOTTOM RIGHT: Earth Lead Animators (LEFT TO RIGHT): *Richard Bazley (Amphitryon and Alcmene), Ellen Woodbury (Pegasus), Oskar Urretabizkaia (Hydra), Chris Bailey (Nessus), Ken Duncan (Megara), Andreas Deja (Hercules), Eric Goldberg (Phil), Randy Haycock (baby and young Hercules).*

Olympus

Zeus, Hera: Tony DeRosa

Tony DeRosa came to Disney from New Jersey via CalArts. His first job as lead animator was on Bernard in *The Rescuers Down Under*. For *Hercules* he is animating the king and queen of Olympus, Zeus and Hera. Using the Scarfe drawings as inspiration, DeRosa has given Hera an elongated art deco appearance.

"The gods and goddesses get that long, bigger-than-life feeling, almost like fashion model proportions, very tall and slender," he explains.

DeRosa points out the large Scarfe drawing of Zeus over his table. "You can see by the hair design and other things that it has to be simplified a little bit," he says. "You could never animate all the curls without going crazy."

ABOVE: *Olympus Lead Animators, left to right: Tony DeRosa (Zeus and Hera), Mike Swofford (Hermes), Mike Show (The Muses).*

TOP: *Concept art of Olympus by Tom Cardone.*

LEFT: *Concept art of Zeus by Tony DeRosa.*

BELOW: *Storyboard art of Baby Hercules and Zeus by Mark Kennedy.*

ZEUS

Oh, he's strong—like his dad.

HERCULES
PROD. #1461
RUFF MODEL SHEET
DATE 11/11 95
APPROVAL
RC

ZEUS #6

ABOVE: *Model sheet of Zeus by Lead Animator Tony DeRosa.*

BELOW: *Rough animation of Hera by Tony DeRosa.*

The Zeus of Disney's *Hercules* is not the angry tosser of lightning bolts so often depicted in other versions. As Hercules's father, he needed to have a warmth and tenderness about him. He is still the king of the gods, but a benevolent one, secure in his own strength. Only in the finale, when Hades is attacking Olympus, does he assert his power.

DeRosa drew from many sources for the body of Zeus. The Greek myths pictured Zeus as an older, powerfully built man, and DeRosa opted for a strong, muscular body. After experimenting with costumes with a collar and sleeves, DeRosa opted for clothing that would expose the character's powerful upper body so his musculature could be more visible. Early Greek art depicts Zeus and other gods wearing loose fabrics.

"I always thought of Zeus's hair as clouds, so I drew it a bit billowy and flowing. I think the Michelangelo Sistine Chapel painting of God transferring life to Adam has a sense of that as well. The hair, the strong upper body—it's very similar. Same concept with a different take on it."

DeRosa often listened to the soundtrack of Rip Torn, who voices Zeus. "The combination of a commanding king and a loving father provides a good balance."

Likewise, Samantha Eggar's voice helped in the animation of Hera.

"I see her as always moving in an ethereal manner," says DeRosa. "Her hair is always kind of floating, and the sleeve has a flowing movement."

Comments DeRosa: "I'm enjoying working on Hera; it's a different type of challenge with her. She's more feminine, more delicate in the acting, yet she's different from the women you would have on Earth. She's a goddess."

Muses: Mike Show

A Greek chorus that sings spirituals is one way to describe what Mike Show is creating for *Hercules*. The film's Muses—Comedy, Tragedy, History, Music and Dance—are unlike any muses previously depicted in sculpture.

"Instead of the traditional, standing-upright Greek chorus, they're more the singing, dancing, gospel, bluesy Greek chorus," explains Show, a CalArts graduate and native of Minnesota. "They move and swing and sass—unlike traditional Greek choruses.

"They exist like drawings on a flat wall or as statues. They don't exist in the world with the other characters. You can put them on a wall, make a statue out of them, a bust, or on a plate. So when they're talking and singing, they have little design elements all around. They live in their own realm, their own two-dimensional graphic world."

The Muses became who they are during a long developmental stage. Some on the production reasoned that since the Muses came off a vase, they should look like classic Grecian characters. Show argued that since their voices come from African American singers they should look African American—"you have to believe these voices would come out of these mouths."

Their look became less classical and their sizes varied. Calliope, the Muse of music, became the main narrator, not unlike the lead singer in a rock band. Show describes Thalia, the muse of Comedy, as the plump one. "Those proportions seemed to fit comedy, like Lou Costello or Oliver Hardy."

He described Clio (History) as a prig, Melpomene (Tragedy) steeped in melodrama, and Terpsichore (Dance) as a cutie-pie.

The Muses first appear unmoving on a vase. Once the music starts, they step off and start gyrating—"there's just no standing still."

Animating one character is a huge task. But five?

"It is time-consuming," Show admits. "But these characters are fun."

ABOVE: *Cleanup of the Muses by Merry Clingen, animation by Mike Show.* (LEFT TO RIGHT) *Calliope, Thalia, Clio, Melpomene and Terpsichore.*

BELOW: *Rough animation of Calliope by Mike Show.*

A Remarkable Achievement

The Little Mermaid... Beauty and the Beast... Aladdin... The Lion King... Pocahontas... The Hunchback of Notre Dame... Hercules.

Disney Feature Animation has produced an unbroken procession of innovative and highly successful entertainments. It would be difficult to find any other film organization with such a record. So successful have the films been that several major film companies have founded animation divisions or have upgraded existing ones. The prospect of revenues from theaters, videocassettes, merchandising and other sources is too enticing to resist.

The new enterprises face a daunting task in matching a company that has dominated animation for 65 years. Yet a whole new generation of artists has emerged with an inspiring zest for animation, and they will pursue their art, at Disney or elsewhere. The field grows more exciting with the unfathomed possibilities of computer imagery. The future of animation seems limitless.

Michael Eisner observes:

"Animation allows artists to escape the boundaries of reality and enter a whole new realm of creative exploration.

"Early animators, whose products were frequently comedy cartoon shorts, took advantage of this freedom to suspend the physical laws so that cartoon characters could undergo the most extreme kinds of trial such as falling off mountains, swallowing bowling balls, and being shot from cannons without suffering any permanent damage. Disney's recent cartoon shorts, featuring Roger Rabbit, continue in this tradition, and even longer works take huge liberties with nature's laws to amuse, delight, and captivate the viewer.

"Thus, in *Aladdin* we find the outrageous blue genie assuming dozens of shapes and personalities, while in *Beauty and the Beast* we have an entire household transformed into various pieces of furniture, in *Pocahontas* a talking tree, and in *The Hunchback of Notre Dame* a team of wise-cracking gargoyles.

"Meanwhile, back in the real world of live action filmmaking, where the laws of physics still reign, we find an explosive new fondness for special effects which reflects in some ways an attempt by the live action film community to find the freedom that animators come by so naturally.

"It was Walt Disney who first used animation to convey not only comedy and whimsy but beauty and drama as well, and it has been the company he founded which continues to lead all others in the art and technology of the wonderful creative realm of animated film.

"At Disney, animation is our calling . . . and our commitment. We salute the long line of Disney animators whose work speaks so eloquently."

Glossary of Animation Terms

ANIMATOR .... An artist who makes a successive series of drawings that give the illusion of movement.

APM .... Assistant Production Manager. Manages various departments and reports to the production manager.

AVID .... An electronic editing machine which edits digitized film in a computer.

BACKGROUND .... The opaque painting that serves as the scenery behind the animation.

BREAKDOWN .... An intermediate drawing between the animator's key drawings.

CAPS .... Computer Animation Production System. Disney's Academy Award®-winning system that helps the artists assemble the animation, background, special effects, and computer-animated elements onto the final piece of film.

CEL .... A transparent sheet of celluloid on which an animation drawing is inked and painted.

CGI .... Computer Generated Imagery. Elements of the film that are created by computer animators and technicians—e.g., the Beast's ballroom, the wildebeest stampede, and the magic carpet's pattern in *Aladdin*.

CLEANUP .... The process of refining the lines of rough animation and adding minor details.

COLOR KEY .... A small color sketch that illustrates what a particular scene will look like in the final movie.

CUT .... The point where the scene ends.

DIRECTOR .... Supervisor of the timing, animation, sound, music, and general production processes of a picture.

EDITORIAL .... A department responsible for all of the visual and sound elements on a project.

EFFECTS .... Animation elements other than character animation or special illusions, such as clouds, rain, shadows, lightning, trick shots, effects etc., supporting the main action of the scene.

EXPOSURE SHEET .... A form which details the action, dialogue, and music for a scene. Each line represents a frame of film.

FIELD .... The area actually photographed by the camera.

FLIPPING .... To hold a group of drawings so that they will fall in an even pattern and give the viewer the illusion of movement.

FRAME .... The individual picture on the film; there are sixteen frames to each foot of film, twenty-four frames to each second of running time on the screen.

HOLD .... To keep drawings or other art material stationary for a number of frames.

IN-BETWEENER .... The artist who finishes the needed number of drawings to create the movement in between those created by the assistant animator and the breakdown artist.

INKER .... One who copies drawings onto cels with ink.

LAYOUT .... The black and white rendering done by a layout artist that determines the basic composition of the scene and provides the drawing for the background artist to prepare the final painting.

MOVIEOLA .... A small machine for the viewing of motion picture film.

OFFSTAGE .... Dialogue, narration, or sound effects coming from a source not on the screen.

PAINTER .... One who paints color on cels.

PAN .... A sweeping, panoramic camera shot accomplished by moving art material under the camera.

PEGS .... The round or rectangular pegs that hold animation, cels, layouts and backgrounds in alignment.

REGISTRATION .... To keep drawings, cels, and background in proper relation to each other.

ROUGH .... The animator's sketchy drawings.

SCENE .... A segment of action within a sequence.

SEQUENCE .... A succession of scenes furthering the story line, usually centered on a particular location or action, e.g., the ballroom sequence, the bell tower sequence, or the happy ending sequence.

SEQUENCE DIRECTOR .... A member of the staff of directors, one who handles a sequence or sequences of an animated feature.

SOUND EFFECTS ...... Miscellaneous sounds added to the soundtrack to enhance the action.

STAGING .... The basic visual presentation of a scene or action.

STORYBOARD .... A large board on which sketches and dialogue strips are pinned in consecutive order to tell a story.

STORY SKETCH .... A simple storytelling drawing done by a story artist.

SWEATBOX .... A meeting with the directors and key artists to critique individual scenes in the film. Originally named after Walt Disney's Movieola room which was under a stairway that didn't have any air-conditioning, the meeting is now done in editorial on the AVID.

TAKE .... A strong movement denoting surprise or reaction.

TRUCK .... A move of the camera, either into or away from the art material on the camera table, or the simulation of that movement in the CAPS process.

INDEX

Sandra Johnson

Bob Thomas

Bob Thomas interviewed Walt Disney many times while Hollywood correspondent for Associated Press and in the preparation of two books, *The Art of Animation* and a child's biography, *Walt Disney: Magician of the Movies*. After Disney's death, Thomas wrote the official biography, *Walt Disney: An American Original*.

Thomas is the author of numerous other books, including biographies of Harry Cohn, Irving Thalberg, David O. Selznick, Joan Crawford, William Holden, Walter Winchell, Fred Astaire, and others. His biographies of Howard Hughes and Abbott and Costello became television movies. He continues to report on films for AP.

In 1988, Thomas became the first reporter-author to be honored with a star on Hollywood Boulevard's Walk of Fame. He and his wife, Patricia, live in Encino.